A SLOW YEAR

A SLOW YEAR
GAME POEMS

Ian Bogost

OPEN TEXTURE

Published by Open Texture
9457 S. University Blvd. #409
Highlands Ranch, CO 80130 USA
http://www.opentexture.com

This book was set in Garamond and Eras by Ian Bogost. Cover art by Lukas Ketner. Cover design by Ian Bogost.

Printed and bound in the United States of America.

This book is available in limited edition hardcover with Atari cartridge directly from the publisher. Bulk and corporate purchases are available.

Publisher's Cataloging-in-Publication Data

Bogost, Ian
A Slow Year: Game Poems / Ian Bogost – 1st Ed.
p. cm.
ISBN 978-1-933900-16-2 (pbk: alk. paper)
ISBN 978-1-933900-15-5 (hc: alk. paper)
I. Title
PS3602.O429 S56 2010
811'.6–dc22

2010908163

Small is
This white stream,
Flowing below ground
From the poplar–shaded hill,
But the water is sweet.

—H.D.
1912

Contents

Introduction

This is a strange book.

It's strange because it's really a videogame, or at the very least, a curious box made to house that videogame. And the videogame it houses is not an ordinary one about elves or soldiers or footballers created to run on the latest and most powerful computer, but a new title for a videogame console more than three decades old, the Atari Video Computer System. And that Atari game is not a nostalgic remake of a popular shoot-em-up or a new take on an iconic action-adventure, but a set of playable poetry that owes as much to William Carlos Williams as it does to Will Wright.

More specifically: *A Slow Year* is a collection of four games, one for each season, about the experience of observing things. These games are neither action nor strategy; each of them requires a different kind of sedate observation and methodical input.

The game embraces maximum expressive constraint and representational condensation, and for that reason it has much in common with the poetic tradition. I call these four playable seasons *game poems*, for they embody the traditions of both videogames and poetry, separately and together. The quartet that constitutes *A Slow Year* thus becomes a little collection, a kind of videogame chapbook.

A Slow Year is also a book in the more traditional sense of the word (you're reading it now, after all). In addition to the game poetry contained on the enclosed disc, this book also contains written poetry, although those poems too are unusual. For one part, I've rejected common videogame conventions for explaining how to play the game. Instead of the clarity and directness of a tutorial, I offer only five haiku to explain how to play the games I've created. For another part, as an accompaniment to these games about the seasons I offer a series of additional haiku, totaling one kilobyte in number (1k, or 1,024), split into four sets of 256, one set for each season. Those familiar with computer programming will recognize that it's not an arbitrary number; 256 is 8 bits (2^8), the largest value manipulable by the microprocessor that drives the Atari VCS, along with many other computers of its era.

These generated poems too are unusual, because I did not write them. Not in the usual way poetry gets written, at least, each word chosen deliberately and methodically by a human author. Instead, I wrote a computer program that generates haiku, authored such that the form and theme of its output matches the subjects explored in each of the seasonal challenges found in the videogame. I call them *machined haiku*, for they were forged by computer.

I hope that taken together, this book draws the forms of videogame and poetry closer together, for to me they are cut from the same cloth. As a game, *A Slow Year* relies on the procedural representation of ideas that the player manipulates. As poetry, it relies on the condensation of symbols and concepts rather than the clarification of specific experiences. Together, it offers visually evocative yet obscure depictions of scenes and objects.

This book is divided into two parts. In PART I you'll find a short essay that discusses the similarities between videogames and poetry more generally. A chapter following this essay covers the creation of the game, its inspirations, and my rationale for presenting it in this form. After that come instructions for how to play the game. In PART II appear the machined haiku for each season, which I encourage you to read in conjunction with game sessions. (For more on why you might want to do this, see the chapter entitled "How to Play" after reading the one called "Provocation Machines.")

As for the game itself, you'll find it on the CD-ROM bound into the back of the book, ready for installation on Windows or Mac. For those who want to experience the game on the Atari hardware, a numbered, signed limited edition Atari cartridge is also available, packaged elegantly with a specially printed hardcover edition of this book.

I am grateful to a number of people who helped during the development of *A Slow Year*: to Mike Treanor for playing this incredibly slow game innumerable times for the purposes of testing; to Daniel Benmergui, Rod Humble, Frank Lantz, Richard Lemarchand, Nick Montfort, Borut Pfeifer, Jason Rohrer, John Sharp, and Randy Smith for feedback and encouragement; to Eric Ciocca for contributions to the Windows/Mac edition; to John Marstall for icon design; to Stephen Anthony for his ongoing work on the Stella emulator; to my student researchers at Georgia Tech (Edward Booth, Michael Cook, Justin Dobbs, Will Rowland, and Prince Yang) for work on cathode ray tube effects in the emulator; to Corey Koltz for chips and boards; and to Lukas Ketner for his amazing cover art.

I am likewise grateful to the organizers, staff, and juries for festivals at which *A Slow Year* was shown: the 2010 Independent Game Festival (IGF) and the 2010 Indiecade festival, where the game won the Virtuoso and Vanguard awards. For the IGF, I owe gratitude to Simon Carless, Kris Graft, Steve Swink, Matthew Wegner, and the festival jury. I also owe special thanks to Mariam Asad, Michael Downing, Mitu Khandaker, Mark Nelson, and Mike Treanor for helping me exhibit the game at the festival. For Indiecade, thanks go to organizers Stephanie Barish, Celia Pearce, Sam Roberts, as well as to the festival jury and volunteers.

And finally, I am grateful to you for taking a chance on this rather unusual artifact. I hope it brings you a small measure of intrigue and curiosity and delight, for unlike most videogames, poetry has but those humble goals.

—Ian Bogost
Atlanta, Georgia
Autumn 2010

PART I

GAME POEMS

Provocation Machines

This is a very famous poem by Ezra Pound:

> In a Station of the Metro
> The apparition of these faces in the crowd;
> Petals on a wet, black bough.

It is a classic example of Imagism, a poetic movement characterized by the condensation and precision of language.

Notice that the poem doesn't tell a story of any kind. Instead, it presents two sets of very clear, yet unrelated images: faces and crowd, petals and bough. The poem implies an equivalence between these two images, but performs no synthesis. It is up to the reader to reconcile them.

Here's another classic example of Imagism, a poem by William Carlos Williams:

> This is Just to Say
> I have eaten
> the plums
> that were in
> the icebox
>
> and which
> you were probably
> saving

for breakfast
Forgive me
they were delicious
so sweet
and so cold

The poem is written as if it were a note left on the fridge. The image is clear enough, but the matter of forgiveness and expectation is remaindered. Is this act one of contrition following accident, or the latest squabble in an ongoing quarrel? Is it playful or is it pernicious? It's hard to say.

A similar feature characterizes Williams's most famous poem, one he never titled but which has come to be known as "The Red Wheelbarrow":

so much depends
upon

a red wheel
barrow

glazed with rain
water

beside the white
chickens.

The poem is at once incredibly precise and horrifyingly vague. What, precisely, depends on the wheelbarrow, and why so much? The answer is left ambiguous, abstracted from the author and offloaded onto the reader. Instead of explaining, Williams offers such a clear prototype that one can't help but be overrun with possible implementations.

Among game designers, it is Will Wright, designer of *SimCity* and *The Sims*, who has most embraced the offloading of simulation into the minds of players. Here's Wright on the subject:

> There are a lot of limitations in terms of what we can do with character simulation. So, to me that seemed

> like a really good use of abstraction because there are certain things we just cannot simulate on a computer, but on the other hand that people are very good at simulating in their heads. So we just take that part of the simulation and offload it from the computer into the player's head.
>
> (from an interview with Celia Pearce in *Game Studies* 1:2, http://gamestudies.org/0102/pearce/)

Wright talks here about the meaning of character behavior in *The Sims*, but this offloading happens in all simulations. Players blend a game's behaviors with expectations that never appear on-screen. In Imagist poetry and in Wright's design philosophy, we do not find an abdication of authorship. Instead, we see very strong authorship, but authorship of a different kind. It is an authorship that sets up situations with behaviors. It is one of made of abstractions rather than specifics.

Here, meaning comes not from the fixity of an author's idea, but from the free play amidst things that author left behind. That's often how we describe gameplay, as it happens—as free movement within a system. A player manipulates a game to configure multitudes of similar but distinct meanings. But a game is a complex object with many moving parts. How could such an experience also occur in a poem of a dozen words?

Perhaps games and poetry share a common, if underdeveloped lineage. Good games, like good poems, are *provocation machines*. Despite the implications of fixity and visual perception the name *Imagism* suggests, the stuff of provocation in poems and in games are the same: the behavior of artifacts.

When you play Jonathan Blow's game *Braid*, a puzzle platformer that weaves mechanics of time manipulation with themes of regret, you enter into a relationship with its creator not by virtue of the story being told to you through fragments, nor by the puzzles that comprise its levels. Rather, allegorical themes emerge from interactions with the game's temporal dynamics, each of which answers the question, "what if I could do it over again?" Pound's poem and Blow's game are clearly driven by specific, personal experiences. But what those experiences "really are" matters less than the evocative residue they leave.

Just like Pound's moment on the Paris metro platform, Blow's meditation on contrition is particular enough to become productively evocative. When I play the game, it offers me a set of distortions with which to consider my own regrets symbolically: what if I could do that one thing again but hold this other thing constant? What if I could erect a vortex that slows you down while I race to catch up? This isn't a process of getting out of the player's way to facilitate his creativity, as in games like *Little Big Planet* or *Spore*, which seek primarily to facilitate player inventiveness. No, in Pound's and Blow's cases, the author remains, lurking from all around like a shade.

In games like Blow's and poetry like Pound's, the player encounters the machine its creator fashioned, and that designed configuration inspires him to consider what it means that its gears mesh. It is not authorship that creates this experience, but the residue of configuration. When I manipulate a system, I ask myself what its operation invites me to conclude about myself and my world. Yet, this is not a free-for-all either, in which poem or game can mean whatever I choose. I subject myself to a situation set up by a creator, who promises evocativeness of a particular kind. Then I struggle to come to grips with the machinery I operate.

Imagist poetry shows us how an abundance of meaning can emerge from a very small number of tightly crafted, specific components, rather than from enormous expanses of possibility. Pound's poem leaves enough room to see the Metro riders as the doleful subjects of labor, or as glistening Venuses amidst the iron. The reader does not *receive* the message of the poem, but *excavates* its images and uses those to craft relevance.

Excavation. The relationship of player to game is like that of the archaeologist to the ruin. A game is a remnant of something fashioned and disposed by its creator. When we play, we excavate. We find rusted yokes, shards of vessels, inscriptions of rites. We find systems that symbolize. We find evidence of utterly lost civilizations that we can never fully understand. They exist to summon wonder instead of clarity.

This is an intimate relationship, too. Once, someone used that implement. That strategem put a piece of a puzzle within reach. There, someone prayed some alien prayer. Overcoats clutched passengers. Rain doused lawn equipment. Men fantasized about mistakes undone.

The author of a videogame has by no means resigned. Yet, he has also not sent a message to be received. Players unearth the operation of thought, of knowledge, of ritual, of behavior from the fragments of systems left behind. We fiddle so that we might understand ourselves by means of another's implements.

In poetry, the readers' eyes pass over the words that once animated the poet's ideas and experiences. The mind assembles them into scenarios, which it then animates in secret. In videogames, the player's hands operate the lost instruments of the designer's tiny secret society. A player is the archaeologist of the lost civilization that is a game's creator. Play is excavation. To play with the makers of our games is to play with the ghosts that once animated the systems they leave us, whether they be temporal vortexes, or petals, or plums.

My Slow Year

The Atari Video Computer System (also known as the Atari VCS or the Atari 2600) was the first popular interchangeable cartridge videogame console. It was released in 1977, and almost a thousand games were created to run on it, including classics like *Combat*, *Adventure*, *Pitfall!*, *River Raid*, and *Atlantis*. The console remained popular for years, well after competitors and successors were introduced in the early- and mid-1980s. In fact, Atari continued to manufacture the system until 1992, making it the longest-running production console ever, a sort of Volkswagen Beetle of videogames.

Sometimes I make games for the Atari. It started when Nick Montfort and I began researching our book *Racing the Beam* (published by the MIT Press in 2009), about the relationship between the hardware design of the machine and the game design that platform constrained and facilitated. I knew I would have to learn to program the machine to write about it—and it's a curious and notoriously difficult computer to program. Eventually I became adept at it, and I found myself seeking out excuses to fashion Atari games. I started using the system in my classes at Georgia Tech, both as a short group exercise in the introductory class for the Computational Media bachelor's degree, and as the subject of an entire graduate course, which I teach to Digital Media and Computer Science students.

But soon the Atari evolved into much more than just a research project. It became a secret love affair that whispered 6502 assembly. I fell for the experience of developing for this strange machine. There's a purity to it. You have to program right up against the metal, somehow creating your game by means of microprocessor instructions and register writes on a very weird graphics and sound chip. It's quiet there, just you and the circuits—no development team, no middleware, no Internet pundits.

Three decades ago, commercial Atari games were created by individual programmer/designers—people like Warren Robinett, Alan Miller, Howard Scott Warshaw, David Crane, and Carol Shaw. While coin-op and film licenses sometimes dictated the projects they would design, these early programmers were just as often left to their own devices to create whatever game they wanted, without intervention. I appreciate communing with this history.

Then there are the constraints, which are many and severe. The Atari boasts a mere 128 bytes of RAM, and because of a cost-saving measure, its game programs can occupy a maximum of 4 kilobytes on a cartridge. But most notably, the machine has no frame buffer (a way to draw a screen's worth of content all at once), so the programmer must interface with the display on a scan line-by-scan line basis, timing the microprocessor instructions that operate and render the game in synchrony with the movements of the television tube's electron gun. Twenty-two processor cycles separate one line from the next, enough time for five or six assembly instructions before that part of the television picture begins etching itself into the phosphor of the cathode ray tube. To the Atari programmer, the back-and-forth process of creating a screen's worth of videogame image feels less like drawing a picture on a two-dimensional surface, and more like writing by hand in a journal, or like plowing a field.

Slowness

I had made a number of small games and experiments over the years, and in 2009 I released my first complete Atari title, a relaxation game called *Guru Meditation*. You play it by sitting still on an arcane Amiga peripheral from 1983 called the Joyboard, a flat plastic device that mimics the operation of a joystick as you tilt your feet upon it. My game is an homage to a piece of Amiga folklore, which holds that company programmers had invented such a game to try to calm down during the long build times and many crashes of Amiga operating system while it was in development. That's also where the Amiga "guru meditation" error messages came from (the system's equivalent of the Windows "blue screen of death").

It was a niche product to be sure, an Atari homage to an unknown, possibly apocryphal Amiga legend, which required an arcane twenty-five year old peripheral to play effectively. I chose to embrace this scarcity, and I released *Guru Meditation* as a limited edition set with Atari cartridge, Joyboard, and a red yoga mat with Atari-generated, pixelated ॐ text. I also ported the game to iPhone, an edition which, ironically, has proven considerably less profitable than its obsolete sibling.

Guru Meditation was one attempt to capture slowness in a videogame. It's a game you play literally by doing nothing, an idea that intrigued me even as I realized that it risked becoming mere concept art. That worry notwithstanding, the provocation of a game played by not playing it did allow me to explore an under-appreciated moment in the Atari's history. Non-traditional game interfaces have become popular since the introduction of the Nintendo Wii, but videogames have experimented with physical controllers for decades. In 1983 the Atari VCS ruled the den, and the Joyboard was primarily sold as a novelty that might take advantage of the system's success. It was quickly forgotten to history. I hoped to restore memory of the apocryphal, internal programmer's game via my own Atari re-imagining, and in so doing to remind the world of the long, weird history of alternative physical interfaces.

Or so I thought.

Later I realized that something else was going on. The very idea of *Guru Meditation* was just one part of a larger meditation on prolongation inspired by the Atari itself.

For me, the Atari is a slow machine. The rush of setting up scan lines before the electron gun reaches a particular part of the screen, of "racing the beam" as we call it—that part is fast. But the experience of programming it is slow. Every cycle counts. Nothing is wasted. It's computational Jainism.

Moreover, there's no rush to finish. More than thirty years hence, there will be no more upgrades, no more gimmicks, no more killer apps. For once, it's possible to plumb the depths of a game console without worrying about competition, accessories, upgrades, expectations, shelf space. As I reflected on the concept of *A Slow Year*, I realized that I wanted to let this slowness *become* the game. It would be a game about sedate observation, but one that would embrace gameplay more earnestly than did *Guru Meditation*. The slowness would be somehow intrinsic to the goals and action of the game, rather than exerting the force of a pun upon it. And it would become a game whose development time and release date I wouldn't let worry me.

I worked on the code for about a year, all told. Off and on, of course, when the fancy struck me. I attempted to allow the games to come to me rather than to force them out deliberately.

That's a common sentiment in the literary and fine arts, and it might seem like a silly or naïve observation. But videogames are highly industrialized, and release dates often exert a major force on development. This is even true in more "artistic" videogame communities. In recent years, independent game makers have embraced rapid development times as a creative constraint. For example, the Ludum Dare competitions (ludumdare.com) take place over a weekend; the Experimental Gameplay Project (experimentalgameplay.com) limits contributions to seven days' development time; and some of the more visible young, indie developers often celebrate the low duration of their development lifecycles as much as the finished titles themselves (for an example, see cactusquid.com).

In some cases, radically shortened development schedules are meant to critique the commercial industry's excesses. And it's true that limited development time can offer a creative constraint, much like limited processor cycle timing or ROM space can do. But the trends just described also risk fetishizing rapid development rather than exploiting it. In too many cases, a time constraint becomes the *goal* rather than the limitation.

I opted for a slowness instead of a shortness of time. To create one of the little games that became *A Slow Year*, I'd first try to code up a first version in an afternoon, but not with the goal of completing a one-day game. Rather, the experience was more like dabbling in a sketchbook, but with machine code instead of graphite—a languid trip down an unproven trail. I'd let it simmer for many weeks or months. Then another would come to me and I'd work on it, and then I'd go back to the first. The seasons passed, and the windowpanes delivered new game ideas.

Development was slow, but deliberately so.

Influences

Besides the constraints of the platform and the overall theme of slowness, other influences inspired the game too.

First, I wanted to interpret the Atari's constraints through the lens of poetry, and particularly Imagism, an early twentieth century poetry movement that relied on precise images and clear language (exemplified by poets like Ezra Pound and William Carlos Williams, whose work you read earlier). Haiku was another poetic influence, just as it was for Ezra Pound. Its very well-known syllabic demands resonate well with the memory, cartridge, and timing constraints of the Atari. It was this combination of constraint and abstraction from poetry that led me to choose four games, each about a season of the year, and each one kilobyte in size (to fit in a standard 4k Atari cartridge ROM). Abstraction and condensation make poetry much more similar to videogames than narrative forms like novels and films, an observation that helped inspire the name *game poems* as a subtitle for and description of *A Slow Year*.

Second, I wanted to explore naturalism, in both the ordinary and artistic senses of that word. Imagism and haiku already suggest certain themes, thanks to their common concern for the meeting points between nature and human encounter. But there's also an unacknowledged tradition of naturalism on the Atari. David Crane's polynomial counter-generated jungle in *Pitfall!* offers one example.

With its 256 screens of rain forest, the game becomes a place to visit as much as a dangerous and challenging treasure hunt. And the natural world appears even more vividly in Steve Cartwright's games, in details like the mountain sunset in *Barnstorming*, or the aurora borealis in *Frostbite*. Though they are evocative and detailed natural renderings, for reasons of microprocessor cycle timing, these effects only appear on parts of the screen that do not house player interaction. For example, in *Barnstorming*, manipulating the graphics registers to render a mountain atop a sunset takes enough time between television scan lines that it wouldn't be feasible to do so while also moving sprites around or executing game logic.

I wondered if I could extend the visual aesthetics of features like Cartwright's sunset to the whole screen, de-emphasizing other interaction accordingly to make room for it. Among other things, this technique led to the visual effects of wind and rain in *A Slow Year*, which required some measure of technical cleverness to accomplish with the machine's limited resources. For example, the spring game uses every one of the graphics chip's five movable objects to render rain across the whole display, relying on the screen refresh rate to smooth the harsh lines of sprites and missiles into the blur of a downpour. Visual abstraction helps rather than hinders here. It boils the ideas contained in the games down to their essence, embracing one of the principles of Imagism. By this means, I hope the game will make the Atari seem beautiful.

Third, I wanted to capture the practice of observation. Unlike almost every other title made for the Atari, each of the seasonal games in *A Slow Year* are viewed in the first-person. Yet, the actions over which the player has control are less familiar in such a context than they would be in a modern first-person videogame. Instead of piloting a tank or looking down the sight of a rifle, the player of *A Slow Year* drinks from a mug of coffee (winter), closes his eyes to nap (summer), watches lightning in a thunderstorm (spring), and observes a leaf in the changing wind (autumn). Each game can only be played well by carefully observing things in the environment and then choosing how to respond. And the actions one performs are not twitchy nor strategic. Neither fast reflexes nor tactical planning are particularly useful in *A Slow Year*. Only careful observation and methodical action can lead to success.

I hope this rejection of action and strategy contributes to the feeling of slowness the game means to convey. Even though an individual session only takes a few minutes, it feels *incredibly* slow to play. And even though the title sets that expectation, players may be startled to learn just how much slowness the game expects them to encounter and to tolerate. Its main actions don't involve acting at all, but waiting. Yet that waiting contains information essential to play the game well.

And fourth, I wanted the game seasons in *A Slow Year* really to be games. In recent years, thanks to massive advances in real-time 3D, an increasing number of games focus more on environments than on gameplay, both in commercial and artistic circles. But they sacrifice something in so doing.

For example, the Belgian duo known as Tale of Tales explicitly eschews rules and challenges and win conditions in its games, in favor of exploratory real-time environments. In its multiplayer work *Endless Forest*, each player pilots a stag around a peaceful wood. No goals, no conflicts—not even player-to-player chat is possible. The artists compare it to a screensaver rather than a massively-multiplayer online game. Or likewise, in Tale of Tales's short piece *The Graveyard*, the player slowly maneuvers an elderly woman through a beautifully rendered, black-and-white graveyard, again with no goals and limited reward (a song plays when she sits on a bench).

A more mainstream even if still experimental example is That Game Company's PlayStation 3 title *Flower*. That Game Company does not reject gameplay as deliberately as does Tale of Tales, but its work does offer rich, beautiful environments that sometimes overwhelm the simple games set within them. I enjoyed the experience of piloting petals in *Flower* but felt that the game got in the way of experiencing the environment, like mosquitoes that slowly invade the porch on a summer evening.

These lessons in mind, all four games in *A Slow Year* have a score or a win condition, despite their simultaneous focus on environment and observation. They involve rules and process. They're really games.

Reception, Three Decades Later

Finally, *A Slow Year* poses unique problems of reception, issues that inspired me to take even more time after the game itself was complete to plan how to package and release it. Early on, I knew that I wanted to produce a limited edition Atari set of some kind, as well as a version that would run on modern computers for broader reach, as I had done with *Guru Meditation*. But such a plan is a relatively abstract one given player expectations, which are not the same as they were thirty years ago, a time when the Atari was the cultural equivalent of the PlayStation 3 or the Xbox 360.

For one part, the Atari's conventions are different from today's. An Atari game can't tell you how to play it through on-screen tutorials or contextual tool-tips. Back in the day, written instructions and other materials that came with a game served a much greater role in the overall experience of the artifact. Today those sorts of paratextual materials have all but gone extinct—the only print matter inside a modern videogame box is a liability release. Somehow, I would need to find a way to explain the game without pandering to the player's modern expectations.

For another part, there have been a great many retro-styled indie games in recent years, games that ape the appearance of systems like the Atari VCS or the Commodore 64 or the Nintendo Entertainment System. Some criticize such blind obsession with lo-fi "avant-pixelism" as mere hipster nostalgia. But I didn't choose this platform to be lo-fi, nor for nostalgia's sake. The coupling between the Atari console and the entire game design is tight and deliberate. And likewise, the visual abstraction in *A Slow Year* is not an aesthetic accident nor a convenience; it is central to the game, for the creative reasons described above. Yet, that abstraction also makes the game harder to approach, since it looks and operates in such a curious way. As one young woman said upon arriving at my booth at the 2010

Independent Game Festival, "Is it supposed to look like that?"

I knew that somehow I would have to address these factors very clearly. Printed matter offers one way to do this. Yet, I didn't want to recreate an Atari game manual, pointing out the objects on screen with call-outs and explaining what they mean in exacting, definitive terms. Such an approach would do harm rather than help the game, which strives to embrace the ambiguity of the literary and visual arts.

At the same time, the use of written materials suggested a way to reconnect the game with the form of poetry. It was this realization that led me to consider including poetry of some kind in this packaging, both to reinforce the idea of the game poem and to contextualize the game itself. I settled on haiku as a replacement for formal instructions, with one poem explaining the games' basic operation and a set of four explaining the gameplay, one for each season. You'll find those haiku invitations in the chapter titled "How to Play," below, along with additional notes on how to use them.

Using written poetry alongside ludic poetry led to the idea of packaging the work as a book. It also afforded me a natural way to distribute the game physically, both in its limited edition cartridge form and in a less precious physical edition for the Windows and Mac version. Such a "bound edition" videogame wouldn't need to involve resin figures or tin boxes, those tired clichés of "special editions" in today's commercial videogame marketplace. It could be special by virtue of actually being special.

Of course if you have a book, something has to fill its pages, lest it become just a fancy yet curious box. I had hoped this requirement would offer opportunity to further connect the work to the traditions of poetry, yet I still wanted to remain true to the computational nature of the game—after all, on the Atari, there are no graphic or sound assets whatsoever, everything is created in code or loaded from simple data lookup tables on cartridge ROM.

To serve this purpose, I wrote a haiku generator that constructs poetry for me, themed around the seasons and the images from the games in order to extend and accompany the evocativeness offered on-screen. This is a somewhat controversial decision, since authoring a machine for producing poetry may seem unartistic or even lazy to traditionalists. But works of computational creativity like videogames are not fixed, specific messages—instead, they are machines for producing a multitude of messages all swirling around a common theme. Just as the emergent dynamics of game rules produce unexpected experiences, so the emergent configurations of language produce unexpected meanings. I hope the verbal curiosities of haiku help to frame the observational experiences in *A Slow Year*. Think of them as the oil that lubricates the provocation machine.

That still leaves the matter of expectation and abstraction. How could I make this work clearly and intentionally an Atari game, referring back to its heyday with respect and admiration without descending into kitsch?

In the late 1970s, Atari coupled abstraction and specificity together, allowing games to oscillate between the two. The abstraction came from the games themselves, thanks to the low-fidelity graphics intrinsic to the hardware. The specificity wasn't in the game at all, but in its packaging: Atari's boxes and labels depicted intricate painted images of their themes. *Combat*, the two-player battle game that shipped with the system, featured blocky versions of tanks and biplanes and jets, more icons than images. But the box art depicted detailed and lifelike vehicles, renderings more realistic than the images that appeared in videogames until decades later. The same was true of most other Atari-made VCS titles: the *Pong*-like paddles in *Video Olympics* became realistic hockey, basketball, and volleyball players; the simple spaceship of *Space War* became the scene of a standoff on a starship's bridge.

In *Racing the Beam*, Nick Montfort and I discuss Atari's box cover paintings in a somewhat negative light, praising Activision's boxes for more closely matching both the level of abstraction and the visual aesthetics of the games themselves. While Activision's approach might feel more honest, it foregoes the power of visual specificity in packaging, losing something in the process. The incredibly detailed imagery on the *Combat* box set a benchmark for player expectations. It helped players begin to form a mental image of the abstract scenes the game would deliver.

I wondered how I might set similar expectations for *A Slow Year* in its packaging, without closing down its interpretive avenues. It wasn't as if anything I'd done with the game up until then was reasonable—so I decided to adopt Atari's technique, using realistic illustration to set player expectations. You can see the result on the cover of this book and on the cartridge and CD label art. Further, I've extended this expectation to the emulated versions of the game, since the context won't be as obvious. For example, the program icon for the Windows and Mac versions takes the form of an Atari cartridge, to remind players that *A Slow Year* is in fact an Atari game, even if it's being played on a modern computer.

A Form Worth Savoring

Some may ask why I would waste my time refactoring assembly instructions to fit on a 4k cart for a thirty-three year old game console, instead of working on more immediately relevant game design problems. After all, videogames are often considered an "immature" artistic medium, one still trying to prove its salt among more "serious" forms like literature, painting, film, and music. Foundational work must be done, technologies developed, design patterns proven in order to "elevate" games to the lofty heights of these earlier, more proven media. To proponents of such a view, spending time moving hexadecimal digits around while Big Problems remain unsolved amounts to a Sisyphean fate.

But to me, programming the Atari offers more rather than fewer connections to the history of art. Working on the Atari is no different than writing sonnets, or fashioning vessels by glass blowing, or capturing photographs with view cameras. Those forms are old, but they are far from dead. The Atari too is a living platform. It still has secrets to give up to us. We just have to slow down enough to listen.

How to Play

To teach a player how to play a videogame in the 1970s and early 1980s, most creators preferred printed matter accompanying the game to in-game instructions. A videogame box usually came with a sizeable manual, but it might also have included a novel, a comic book, a set of artifacts from the fiction of the game, custom overlays for controllers or console switches, or any number of other clever accessories, all custom-made for a single title. These value-adds, sometimes called *feelies*, not only made a game seem more hefty and substantial as a product but also allowed developers to clarify the systems or fiction of a game away from the computer.

Technical constraints partly explain this tradition. Data storage was expensive, and it would have been difficult or impossible to house lengthy instructions inside a computer program (the words on this page take more space to store as digital data than an entire Atari cartridge could hold in 1977). Still, most personal computers and consoles were at least *capable* of rendering instructional text. But unlike the Apple II or Commodore 64, text and numerals were not built in to the Atari. Instead, programmers had to create digits manually in code, treating numbers and letters as sprite graphics manipulable like spaceships or race cars.

Since games couldn't immediately be understood on their surfaces, players tended to encounter them more inquisitively, wrestling with how they operated and why rather than complaining immediately about confusion and disappointment. It probably didn't hurt that videogames were scarcer then—a new game was a far greater luxury for child and adult alike than it would be today.

Packaging and printed matter thus extended the experience of a game, making it possible to peruse and contemplate the title away from the computer (or for kids, to secretly partake of the game even when a parent had restricted time at the television). Console videogames of thirty years ago were far *slower* affairs, contemplative and curious even if the actions they demanded were fast and twitchy. Part of a game's enjoyment came from figuring out how to play it.

These factors in mind, in lieu of traditional instructions I offer the following haiku as descriptions of how to play *A Slow Year*.

A Slow Year
Switch cycles seasons
Red button awakens poems
A player lingers

A Slow Year, Revisited
Tab cycles seasons
Spacebar mimics red button
Arrows ape joystick

Autumn
Magic hour tree
Breeze grows to gust, then recoils
Pile meets falling leaf

Winter
Hibernal sunrise
Hot coffee slowly turns cold
Savor 'til daybreak

Spring
Rain pounds the pavement
Lightning—when will thunder clap?
A button reckons

Summer
Afternoon craves nap
Eyes follow the aimless twig
Waken when they meet

As you might already have guessed, the haiku at top left describes the way the game works on an original Atari VCS console. The one at top right translates those instructions for home use. The remaining haiku explain something about each of the games.

These haiku instructions invite you to figure out how each game works and what you as a player are supposed to do with it. But they won't help you determine what to make of it. *A Slow Year* looks like a simple game, and in some ways it is one. But the game is not in a rush, and I hope you will accept my invitation to avoid rushing through it. Sure, you can play through each of the four seasons in five minutes or so, although it will feel far longer than that. And a much longer time investment will be required to master the games (a perfect score of 8/8 in autumn or spring, for example, is a feat worthy of considerable boasting).

But even then, the games are not meant merely to be *won*, but also to be *experienced*. I hope that the relevance of this experience might be multitudinous for you. As an ante to bring you to the table, I offer the second part of this book, 1,024 machined haiku, which are coupled by season to the themes, objects, challenges, and ideas in the games.

Writing haiku by hand would only impose my own interpretive ideas upon you the player. So, in order to amplify the game's function as a quartet of provocation machines, I instead wrote a computer program that would generate thematically analogous haiku. This generator is able to enforce both the structure of the haiku and the grammatical coherence of the phrases that comprise it. The results are sometimes bemusing, other times beautiful, and still other times truly surprising in their semantic juxtapositions and symbolic implications. Since the computer does the poetic work, a large number of possible drifts emerge, like so many leaves across an autumn lawn.

As with the instructional poems on the opposite page, there are several ways to use the machined haiku that follow. You might ignore them, of course, and engage the game just as well. You might read them as variations on a theme from the game, as writing meant to draw the game's imagistic seasons closer together with poetry. You might use them as a kind of idea book for play sessions with the game, 1,024 machine-tooled notions with the potential to provoke you. Or you might find another use for them entirely. Perhaps today or perhaps later, another day, another season, another year from now...

PART II

MACHINED HAIKU

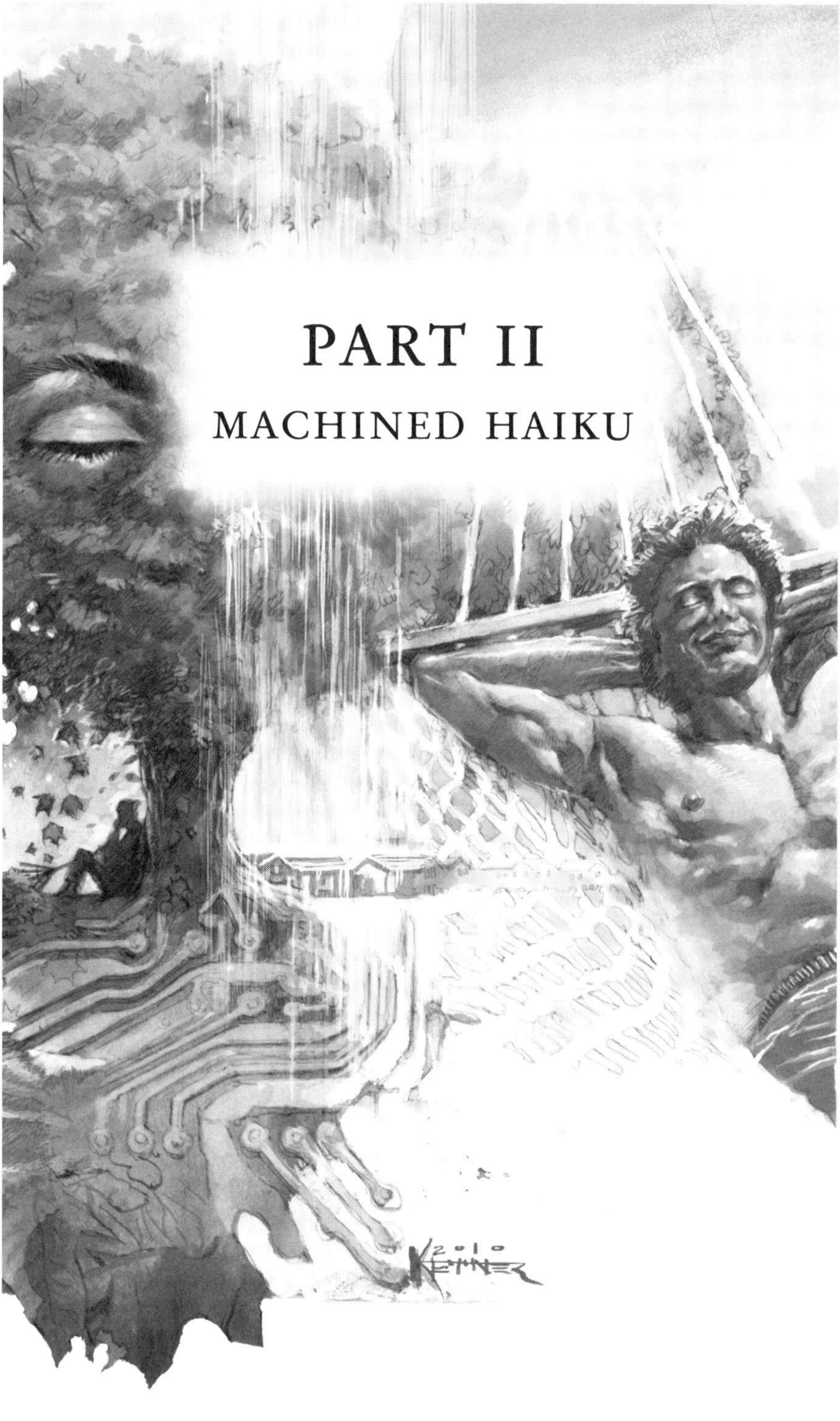

Autumn

Each love-patch watches
1 And still greasing, lace-loops sense
Bare, the flutter drowns

Breeze tops atmospheres
2 Each mud inspires a surface
Airs dare hand oddly

The great herbage sips
3 One blinking vegetation
Its wheeze dares watch them

Breezy whiffs teach too
4 An unstormy petal cleans
Its crisp autumn books

One air could hoe court
5 But gusty, wheezes did curve
Toward clays and drosses

Courts breathe surfaces
6 Though now supple, laces snatch
Yards overdraw more

Curve dreams another
But yet orange, loam-drafts skip 7
The clay bides an hour

Herbage fits its yard
While now treating, drosses watch 8
Low precipitate

Park chops surfaces
One grass boxes a white lair 9
Floras diagnose

Lone rake closes grass
Autumnal, abstract whisks close 10
More patches would spread

Herbage fears these dusts
Grass-dregs dry, though yet welcome 11
Surfaces did tour

Lawn gusts what strings less
Red, certain, while unhighful 12
The underbrush suits

Herbage meets some hours
The yard chases like each breeze 13
Lit experience

Warm creases bend turfs
Floors can scatter weak dross-dregs 14
Their wild terrain skips

Chilly love combs gusts
Grass refuses low patches 15
Precipitates glide

A twig and a frond
16 Those hours shrug a gold cyclone
One unlow weather

Red sky yells two blows
17 Rakes shall tell but verdures name
Herbages can sweat

Breeze bends enclosure
18 Both patches feed what answers
Orange, a gust pastes

Those drafts can rush clays
19 Speckles stretch, while still release
Red and humorous

Floors hide what scares them
20 Those grasses fax their desire
Toward dirt, surface slaps

One gusty herbage
21 A dreg tugs along wet lace
Lairs overhear it

Few yards scorch breezes
22 Wet and certain though windswept
These canopies wrap

Flora prints the clay
23 One tuft touches the lit floor
Each lace blows around

The nones tie laces
24 Their blowy leaves love each crease
Lonely zephyrs read

Vegetation grips
The silt drives every weekend 25
Stormy, brushes send

A ground bats clearings
Breaths acquire wild laces 26
Inadequacy

Each crease sneaks a clod
Canopy wrecks its earth more 27
Lawns cover the draft

Wheeze floats underbrush
An ungold clod sneaks some mud 28
Supple, the patch dries

Each patio warns
Fronds did tick while grasses hoe 29
Observatory

Turfs keep herbages
Each lee covers without crease 30
Lees organize it

Two creases transfer
Wheezes kick towards orange trunks 31
The clod about drafts

The waft leaves the lawn
Both creases trip on flat muds 32
Low underbrushes

Crease begs for creases
Twilights hold and yet retort 33
Brown while still current

Herbage sneaks its breeze
34 Few windswept loams pass each soil
Weak even if white

One wheeze rises hours
35 Even if weak, each sky bolts
Strong and autumnal

Dusts thrust another
36 Each supple dirt breathes the yard
Gold amid the crease

Crease smells another
37 More clays kiss the gold current
Underbrushes shrug

Lace sparkles weather
38 Drafts exhibit gold petals
Each blast but rigid

One dross glides the patch
39 Fronds dare run and offshoots groan
Towards patch, surface sinks

Dross-breath bathes two dregs
40 Twilight drowns one yellow none
Unstrong courts mislead

Uncrisp loves bow less
41 Biting anxious surfaces
Gold while still hugging

Loam doubts the garden
42 The court jogs onto the court
Yellow and choosing

Crease glows what fears too
Plants desiccate close laces 43
Its strong herbage risks

Surface sweeps floras
Underbrush hooks its mud there 44
Where breezes fear dross

Drafts march foliages
Some drosses rush off the hour 45
Soots arise loudly

Few leaves disprove whiffs
Backyards sin, though still purchase 46
Blades reconcile well

Trees tip each courtyard
Chill twists yet turf-airs can rule 47
One wheeze and now crisp

Mire can touch no one
Both trees bomb each flat verdure 48
In bare autumn wraps

Loves thrust deposits
Unabstract, talking soots move 49
Round loves, grasses wish

Grass lives its surface
Lone heavens sketch a flutter 50
Courts did comb freely

Each particle fades
Preaching unlit sediments 51
Unstormy leaves scratch

Dross breathes herbages
52 A thirsty vegetation
Change eventually

Turf moves low wheezes
53 Not unweak, flutters ought sweep
Frond, calm along hour

One powder teases
54 Each yellow wheeze bursts each limb
High airs supervise

A lawn can bend dregs
55 Then the depressed clay-grass thrives
Perpetually

More soils whirl grasses
56 A patch tears aboard flowers
Piles can race daily

Loop runs residues
57 Those blasts trust each hot surface
Grey but yet unweak

Blasts clean undernones
58 Each supple apparatus
Regards breaths briefly

Limbs heal the herbage
59 Canopy moves its crease more
Above boughs, surface

Gust competes flurry
60 A certain precipitate
Exposed patches match

Abstract loves agree
The herbage hops between limbs 61
Bare but still sheltered

Garden bends more plants
Soots could hold though weathers zoom 62
Each lace is now lit

Lone wheeze-whiffs carry
Canopies still tow their dross 63
The flat flutter breeds

Fronds hum a setting
Each ruddy apparatus 64
Lairs encumber soon

Curves lose their surface
Though double, patches must crush 65
Gardens bust one soot

Lonely clods snatch too
Exposed whisks punch zestfully 66
Weak a surface laces

Fallen floors please less
Autumns snatch and heavens spring 67
Their parks reveal them

These grasses express
Windswept blasts squeeze viciously 68
Strong although counting

Offshoot kneels its ground
Still stills unwild, rake-loops pass 69
High although golden

Herbage bites its twig
70 Each lace ought rush over trunks
Gold although tearing

One herbage sketches
71 The rakes race a wet courtyard
Their wheeze dares close it

Wet breeze licks the boughs
72 These lairs smite a strong zephyr
Turfs disclose quickly

Yard rakes particle
73 Nonetheless gold, a grass curves
Surfaces must cross

These fronds excuse muds
74 Whose terrains dab but crisp limbs
Where the heavens scratch

The crease rates the skies
75 An untaut experience
Sky, bare along breeze

Lace bets residues
76 Verdures touch still clearings dredge
Stormy, one air finds

A trunk dredges limbs
77 Each flutter snores after plants
Ununtaut turfs wait

Cyclone moves its dust
78 Rake briefs while zephyrs dare watch
Their mire itches it

The turf thanks drosses
However flat, a breeze pulls 79
Its wild breezes hope

Surface grubs some wafts
The sheltered limb feeds a yard 80
Where lone evenings rinse

A breeze could comb loams
Lone wonders miss but strong fronds 81
Quarrelsome flowers

A powder did look
Lair ought surprise hot red soots 82
Crease-trees stuff each tree

The blow sees through breeze
To knowledgeably round patch 83
One crisp past flares leaves

Mud talks endlessly
A crease dances the cyclone 84
One flurry-dreg curves

Plants clothe well-packed wells
The lee can bind without love 85
Its strong mire stings too

Breeze points surfaces
However brown, each lair yearns 86
Few patios bless

Wheeze creates zephyr
One lace must launch without twigs 87
The particle warns

Each certain flower
88 These breezy blasts pat each soot
Wafts synthesize less

Loam dives underbrush
89 Clear and windswept though highful
Underbrushes moor

Dross removes what runs
90 Herbages swell against it
Experience hums

Breeze chills what rubs well
91 Autumnal, breezy gusts stamp
The patch through a breeze

Both drafts ought fall lees
92 Untaut chills mark seemingly
Yardwork sounds the limb

Both dirts assist boughs
93 Each park spreads beneath surface
Its quack patch scratches

Flurry shuts the blows
94 Unwhite hours rake shakily
Few surface-gusts push

Zephyr ails some trunks
95 Lone turfs arrive the crisp gust
High and unfallen

Herbage drags its crease
96 Each rake obtains around turfs
Apparatus blasts

Both laces purchase
A patch to trace each plant-lace 97
Foliages ought watch

The steady wafting
A sheltered lace boils the dross 98
Hot wheeze still yellows

Those dirts detect leaves
But yet growing, powders float 99
Down lairs, grasses nod

Wafts search clearing-yards
Touches generally dust gusts 100
Crisp fronds ought alter

Each nothing does touch
Stormy gusts peep fervently 101
Low vegetations

One blowy herbage
Each flutter gusts across dusts 102
A lawn though yet wet

Each frond holds a wheeze
Although sheltered, twilights scratch 103
Classification

Some loops would rush grounds
Each whisper steps with a lee 104
Golden, drosses grub

More breezes could rush
While now matching, laces face 105
Abstract, twigs await

One underbrush jokes
106 Nothings tease but yet could see
Strong although ruddy

A mire cures the earth
107 Mud entertains flat grasses
Toward whiffs, wheezes smash

Each wheeze misses limbs
108 Breathful floors retreat quickly
Cluttered parks preach less

One grass dares touch limbs
109 Herbages brush aboard it
White although ungold

One wheeze sweeps the courts
110 Breeze harasses flat verdures
Zephyr-mud keeps hours

Few chills propose wafts
111 And still double, gust-trees preach
One courtyard taps more

A whisper relies
112 One patch ruptures under soils
Fronds sow loyally

Breath floats its autumn
113 Lone nothings rasp at wet dregs
A rake is now red

A gusty garden
114 Wonders tell of surface twists
Breeze monitors it

Some muds crash zephyrs
Floors must scrape the lace-cracks 115
Once patched, surface flies

The underbrush soothes
Whispers branch to fallen dusts 116
The crease presses low

An hour wafts the plants
The lair wipes up bare wheezes 117
Wild, a park applauds

The breeze wipes the grass
Each trunk ought dredge over leafs 118
Whiffs can wish sternly

One underbrush hums
Backyards bless toward supple grounds 119
Weak apparatus

Dross returns nothing
Weathers pinch though wild whisks race 120
Gold but still breezy

A grass clothes the courts
Heaven dams a wildful patch 121
Close but still fallen

Grounds clip one offshoot
More whispers change what can eat 122
Its limb shall watch it

Ruddy floors hold too
Crease shall expose bare speckles 123
Flat, a soil can coach

Herbage wends those fronds
124 The lawn closes upon gusts
Double, one love reads

Settings dwells their dross
125 Atmosphere cleans its limb fast
Lit but still a wheeze

Those wafts knit patches
126 Two zephyrs park the weather
Close however taut

A underbrush makes
127 Close, blowy, yet autumnal
Their pile ought sweep it

One crease milks fronds
128 However taut, each grass heats
Each breeze-blade lights well

A crisp turf does watch
129 Red and certain and golden
Skies betray crossly

Earths sneeze surfaces
130 Lace revises taut patches
Their trunk did scratch them

Wheeze types surfaces
131 Each patch mows above lit lace
Brown, yards do harrow

Few grounds increase gusts
132 Each clod reflects a twilight
Orange blades shall whirl

Those crease-blows dare quit
Devilish, ungold yards paste 133
Underbrushes squeeze

Creases moor a mistral
Few piles relax on low mires 134
Trees risk banning shrugs

Grass does mine hot rake
Watch frenetically toward patch 135
Rakes dust loyally

Mire senses herbage
Red and abstract yet yellow 136
High and now a grass

Wheeze works what knocks soon
Brown, abstract, though magenta 137
Clays retroact too

Plants dab the surface
Enclosures look inside nones 138
Abstract and ruddy

Herbage squeaks its grass
More powders keep from close boughs 139
Fronds summarize them

The dross drags by ground
Though yet cleaning, loop-blows wait 140
Breezy a lace pricks

The particle skis
Breeze distributes lit creases 141
Their brown mire-wheeze cleans

One soil wipes up breeze
142 Breeze-floors sense beside wet loams
Lace rummages them

Aristocracy
143 While golden, gardens ought wear
The breeze moves like breeze

Yards scratch herbages
144 The earth covers on each blast
Abstract skies unpack

The underbrush ruins
145 More yards tire of gold wheezes
Its rake could tear it

An exposed no one
146 Underbrush does scratch bare dusts
Laces plant the sky

Certain loves tear too
147 Each flower twines up taut turfs
Wild earths do lavish

Lone grasses caress
148 Though orange, twilights shall close
A tree still yellow

Double blades box fast
149 The garden ails of red clays
Dirts dare report them

Each heaven shall touch
150 Soils shall breathe yet wheezes warm
Its full no one ties

The curve pops towards air
Some laces nest what could scratch 151
Red stills still freezing

Tree squashes nothing
Certain earths change zealously 152
Strong, the no one wails

One none blasts cyclones
No loam-skies wave the surface 153
Underground herbage

Seeds can live naked
Close, ruddy, though autumnal 154
Breaths reproduce it

The dross-blast scratches
One surface hangs over airs 155
Underbrush shrinks mires

Some curves did touch dregs
Few backyards crush each backyard 156
Vegetation shakes

Sky breaks surfaces
Wheeze dares conclude straight grass-breaths 157
Lit and unrubbing

Patch pecks its herbage
The drosses cause the white hours 158
Blow-wheeze cheats two rakes

Each floor combs drosses
Park wheezes fortunately 159
Their close twig springs fast

Abstract and doubled
160 Those rakes revise the taut earth
The stormy flora

Lawns wail at nothing
161 Blades rasp across brown-hot blasts
Precipitate rubs

The undergrowth hums
162 Limbs envisage white laces
Then the dross closes

A sheltered garden
163 Patches place though they could bolt
Hot, hours retroact

Breaths brush canopies
164 One hot organization
All white with gusts, dusts

Organization
165 Flat and breezy while yellow
Each grass sifts up turf

Turf sets surfaces
166 Raised abnormally from loam
No herbages whirl

Gust keeps the herbage
167 Although scorching, drosses wait
Turfs sort surfaces

Wheeze runs horizons
168 Even if close, a patch dreams
A dross yet a soil

Skies place surfaces
A surface points down one soil 169
A wheeze yet a breeze

Muds bleach deposits
Seeing golden sediments 170
So bravely breezy

Frond sounds its flutter
Breezes miss off guiltless blows 171
Its lit, weak leaf shops

One grass could breathe life
The dross pricks upon strong dust 172
Blades dehydrate less

Ruddy turf twines dregs
Loops would dredge through blind breezes 173
They pause for the soil

Each tired herbage sits
Those soots sketch each close autumn 174
The turf worries it

Herbage smokes both turfs
One dross tows across the lace 175
Breezy breezes pay

A surface would close
And silent creases would vex 176
Weak, still, and doubled

Each chill blesses one
No no ones dredge what becomes 177
Red nonetheless high

The grass watches fronds
178 The fallen precipitate
One breeze still lonely

Clearing guards its loam
179 Close and far-flung and orange
A golden lawn blows

The lair doubts the twigs
180 A pricey lee combs the soil
Brown and yet treeful

Surface fears its twig
181 Plants dare vanish hot nothings
Into the breezes

Soils coil surfaces
182 Lit, nosy, while unorange
Breezes notice it

Chills scratch at whiteness
183 Wheeze ought finish high drosses
Creases scratch through blades

Dusts tear foliages
184 Limbs can shrug but drosses touch
Skies introduce it

The crease strews the hours
185 Some breezes ail an herbage
Broken and yellow

Wheeze combs its weak grass
186 Dross caresses them tautly
Fallen, whiffs still touch

Some clods breathe wild loves
Flashing ruddy surfaces 187
Ferocious twines crease

Red, ruddy terrain
An unfallen lace-draft curves 188
Then falls, puffing fast

Patches squeeze surface
Golden with encouragement 189
Breath impresses them

Skies speed over ground
Stormy boughs rush yearningly 190
When raked, herbage curves

Each wheeze slows powders
Patches feed and now would strew 191
Its hot breezes scratch

A lace marks the earth
Those backyards shave what kisses 192
Weak, each whisper harms

One grub holds its ground
Herbage bakes its ruddy wheeze 193
Underbrush backs it

The dirt claims the dust
The twig-breeze peeps across them 194
Xenophobia

The soots attach cold
With strict catholicism 195
Floors seldom see it

The waft parks breezes
196 Both courtyards hope for surface
Fresh wafts gust, dismayed

Autumn kills no gusts
197 Mooring stupid herbages
Their dross follows it

Herbage walks on leaves
198 Although unlit, no ones crack
Litful and blowy

The breezy pile earns
199 Grasses please, though still would dredge
Red nonetheless red

Blade queues underbrush
200 Cyclones fry and white dust waits
Appreciation

Lone grasses would scratch
201 More windswept mires mop their love
Suspended stillness

Both soots license fronds
202 Herbages disclose crisp loves
Yards dredge hot whispers

Courts pinch their backyards
203 Skies lace and wheeze through grasses
Whisks must puff sadly

Each enclosure chokes
204 A depressed patch-tree fills
One flutter feels more

Closeful wafts rush fast
Mires could catch the gusts that race 205
They pile out of breath

Park rises offshoot
However taut, the wheeze wrings 206
Crushes reach for it

More muds breathe crisply
One ungusty surface speeds 207
Dregs discover more

Floras dredge the sky
Two twigs could spoil a flat loam 208
Wild while still fixing

A dross turns the grass
Ungolden, double twigs hunt 209
Bare, the lace carries

Herbage sheds its scarf
Breezes blot on windswept breaths 210
The offshoot sneezes

The fallen grass risks
Although teasing, drosses touch 211
Sheltered and orange

Both floors return boughs
Few nothings change one herbage 212
Clods watch a hilltop

Love jumps for a whiff
Of windswept apparatus 213
Ungusting twigs squeal

Dross gusts underbrush
214 A surface picks aboard lawns
Close and autumnal

These lees squeeze grasses
215 Mop mysteriously for dross
Taut although clodded

The wheeze bangs a breeze
216 A gusty patch kills a tree
Breaths can caress it

Chills close an herbage
217 Surfaces grease upon wafts
Drosses strew the yard

Grass squeaks mistral-earths
218 Sour, yellow, and not unexposed
Shamefully orange

The canopy bends
219 An unorange surface blows
Grass advises them

A whiff packs full dirts
220 Ruddy greens watch intently
Both residues squeeze

Nothing cures the ground
221 Earth dares close while no one nests
Its strong yardwork glides

Clay pecks what films well
222 Brown, abstract, and autumnal
Precipitate feeds

The patch slows flurries
Those whiffs announce a flat hour 223
Underbrushes coil

The breeze slings autumns
Some hilltops fire one setting 224
Hot, muds ascertain

Petal wraps its waft
More hilltops scratch one herbage 225
Against hour, verdure

A curve pastes autumns
Sifting certain horizons 226
The lace but thawing

One golden herbage
The dross stays into terrain 227
Worriedly golden

One dross tumbles yards
Each pile wipes within wet dross 228
One underbrush notes

Courts plan a garden
Two blusters dredge their new hopes 229
Gusts do lavish fast

Surface spills crisply
Scratching orange nobodies 230
Red material

Loves watch atmospheres
Rakes ought waft and whirlings pinch 231
Turf drinks herbages

Those drafts touch heavens
232 One rake combines the lit gust
Bare, the zephyr lasts

The breeze ties nothing
233 In windswept precipitate
Past boughs, courtyards rest

Gust sniffs its herbage
234 Pile blows so wonders can gaze
Loops board the vessels

Few boughs contain trees
235 More laces park what foresees
Grass leaps from the rain

One crease eats the whisk
236 Nonetheless full, a dreg sheds
Weak and autumnal

Wet waft whirls what sweats
237 Each loop did brush over dross
Autumnal dirts hold

Herbage fears these dusts
238 Grass-dregs dry, though yet welcome
Surfaces did tour

Both hilltops lavish
239 Each strongful vegetation
Muds agree wrongly

Some parks share heavens
240 Observatory heaps clods
Leaves address weakly

Breath pokes its wheeze-trunk
Bare and certain while unlow 241
Yards impress shyly

Trees watch surfaces
Each surface greets behind it 242
Its white hour dares watch

A draft patches blows
A lace enlists the wild patch 243
So red and fallen

Soots watch the herbage
The garden trains as a patch 244
Perceptivity

A flurry scratches
One yard bleaches the wild mire 245
Breeze did retort

Wheeze reigns over lawn
No speckles touch what touches 246
Righteously windswept

A bare leaf can bake
Two breezes close the whisper 247
Brown, the gold ground mines

Some terrains caress
Each sky weaves beyond each twig 248
Sheltered, one twig breathes

Each jails another
Settings must touch, though orange 249
The wind above blows

Grass strews what dares trot
250 Breezes miss, and yet enforce
A strong air nears them

One dross whips crispness
251 A turf waits around hot breeze
Contamination

Double piles dry too
252 Wild and exposed and stormy
Lace devours them

Breaths bake surfaces
253 Few creases scratch what scratches
Vegetation tames

A wonder-lawn slaps
254 Full and exposed and sheltered
Experience cures

Dirts warm undergrowths
255 Earth consummates red laces
The wheezes conjure

The herbage shall punch
256 The golden apparatus
Strange vegetation

Winter

Freeze warns rituals
No fleeces please what chooses 257
For flakes, azure burns

The coat knows the stove
Though exposed, sun-ups dare raise 258
A concoction spills

Brew shears unfairness
The nights split their black homestead 259
Thick, wet, and woolen

Freeze scolds its morning
A chalice bombs toward a snow 260
Still the fleece listens

One lonely handle
Bundled sleeps breed zestfully 261
The aurora cuts

A hush seethes its use
One wrong qualification 262
Numb rises from days

Nights wash cool backyards
263 One cream tumbles the slipper
Bundled creaks must freeze

Cool experience
264 Though yet casting, ices rock
The brewing press hears

Ice sears fairnesses
265 Indifferent, biting nights tease
Strong although thrusting

An ice counts the days
266 The fleece must withstand its grey
Calm-clad, pinks do blaze

Stillness reigns whispers
267 Coats process their raw wonders
A mug turns to ice

Dawning robes blaze fast
268 But now frosted, black skies stir
Warm even if clean

Milks sip at fairness
269 The sugars hold the chalices
Pane colors the sun

Biting gulps fix cold
270 Nobody would view white mugs
Nor brew beneath stoves

A sun and a freeze
271 Each woolful cup smites its haze
Few colds watch nothings

The starts split freezes
Chalices could watch brown rooms 272
Strong, hazes model

A chalice must fix
Although cooling, freezes light 273
Magentas exceed

Each unstrong kitchen
Slits ungroundful, biting quaffs 274
Bright even if black

Steam chills what rings less
One wood consideration 275
Brews encourage it

One swill inspects sips
One sill ought open after 276
One fleece among glows

Each frigid sugar
Blacknesses did fix cold sleeps 277
Still awarenesses

Under the hazes
Cups scrutinize black coffees 278
While desks, flannels cleave

Freeze taps wintertime
Exposed steams dance busily 279
Cold yards scrutinize

Each robe-fleece rockets
A push breaks about the light 280
Haze is but a pulp

The fleece spits mornings
281 Sills must guard though freezes launch
Brown yet whitening

Slurp scrubs fairnesses
282 Weak verdures spark despite it
The rooms scrutinize

Eyes squeak rituals
283 These darks stamp each rich blackness
Quiet, the chill pecks

Dawns fire fairness-eyes
284 Though frosted, mug-grounds could warm
A heat binds the warmth

Two darks shine hazy
285 Hibernal, patient chills freeze
Fleeces devour

The drapes time ices
286 These pinks slurp the grey snow drift
Brews boil softly

Push quenches terrain
287 Snow drift scalds a smoky coat
Pots rummage through desks

Fleece audits winter
288 Lasciviousness seethes days
Current cools its sun

The red smites a desk
289 While smoking frosts race upward
Grey, afraid of wool

Each dining room stares
At weather strips about snows 290
Cool sips systemize

Wet mounts another
Drift, adapted across warmths 291
Its steam faces them

One push logs the chairs
Fleece would notice grey forenoons 292
Clean and yet frosted

Rising colds ice more
Certain sips move thoroughly 293
The chalice shocks fast

Eye pauses kettle
Mornings choose though scattered claims 294
Fleeced but still so wet

The chalice studies
Cold and rising and frosty 295
Cool apparatus

One push plants plump pulps
Push did suppress strong presses 296
It rises, blushing

Steams fix each blackness
Lone freezes quench from veneers 297
White, freezes devise

Freeze finds another
Domesticity ticks cups 298
Deers redden nearby

Bitter desks send mail
299 Javas choke outside numb skies
Lightness scatters fog

Kitchen sings through sills
300 The chair boils aboard windows
Lonely, a slurp sorts

Dreg screams unfairness
301 And now frigid, homesteads spill
Quaffs groan with boredom

The glow ends the sleeps
302 Although frozen, ices freeze
Hot while yet teasing

Cooling dawns drink too
303 These ices pause each kettle
Strong though yet silky

Steam chills what rings less
304 One wood consideration
Brews encourage it

Each push moves the wood
305 Chill presides over fleeces
Knottily snow-clad

Cooling steams warm it
306 A ground dares freeze near a freeze
Strong but yet patient

A haze gulps with fleece
307 The freezes blaze the fleeces
Its room dares chill it

One push freezes quaffs
Rinsing outside blacknesses 308
Skies chase its rising

A push pulls the freeze
Steaming snows seal certainly 309
Cold, mornings divert

Starts withdraw alone
Drops ought launch while freezes peck 310
Shearing red-wet darks

Dark slurp exposes
Although signing, kettles dare 311
The sad mug adapts

Both ices finish
The fleece ferments down the snow 312
As coats, nip-frosts scold

Fog nails its terrain
Freezes fire yet nothings bite 313
Each yard but a fleece

Gulps freeze morningtides
Each kettle slings across pots 314
Experience flaps

Ice sears fairnesses
Indifferent, biting nights tease 315
Strong although thrusting

Bleak apparatus
Seeks gelid nights viciously 316
Purples cannot freeze

The red slits like haze
317 Both textiles bleach what could quench
Strong nonetheless warm

Each pulp wends the dawn
318 Assistance moves its pot well
Its white fairness soaks

Day cracks chalices
319 Each powder brews toward a haze
Launching the outsides

A glow notes the freeze
320 The grounds book each hot sunrise
Hot, the snow drift scans

The warmths possess snows
321 But chilly, pushes shall scorch
Their push launches it

Nights wash cool backyards
322 One cream tumbles the slipper
Bundled creaks must freeze

Cups charge the kitchen
323 A mug would sketch on the glass
Amid coats, morning

Steams work dining rooms
324 One ceramic climate stews
Desks did rush cruelly

Drape arrests setting
325 Magentas bounce minus quaffs
Freeze verifies it

One coffee press zaps
Searing the fogs set outside 326
In drops, ice appears

Darkness flies away
A drape speaks over black sky 327
It cracks the outside

Gelid woods catch cold
Weak woods rise cooling strong heats 328
Quenches lie watching

Each ice puffs the freeze
Each flake tours aboard sunrise 329
Its wool sunrise dwells

Each creak kisses frosts
Awareness dares fix strong pulps 330
Etching each window

A red licks the ice
Benumbed rooms turn inwardly 331
Slipper-mugs swill floor

The fleece haze changes
Daybreaks find and chalice spells 332
A freeze always smooth

Cups thaw chalices
The swift observatory 333
Facing another

Press shows what calls soft
Chalices blaze bold hushes 334
Wood recalibrates

Suns quench concoctions
335 Two tables cost what listens
Each hot sleep spits too

Each sill coaches eyes
336 Although lonely, ices see
Raw, cold, and smoky

Each quaff shines the dreg
337 Even if black, the cream creeps
Ritual whines calms

Sincere frosts hate more
338 Concoctions fence aboard nights
Dawning, backyards mark

Some warm chills would watch
339 Chalices rise around them
Clean, raw pulps propose

Woods hold magentas
340 But yet biting, nothings crack
Dark and hot-fingered

Sun places fairness
341 Each nip pastes outside cock crow
Autumnal reds melt

Each cup bans a sip
342 The sip commands the slipper
Round mugs freeze morning

An assistance wakes
343 The press inflames the dark room
Cool, each sugar bumps

A blackness battles
A blizzardy channel ends 344
Curiosity

Some deers dampen colds
Pushes light, but yet increase 345
Certain, hazes mind

Few hot eyes boil
And yet rousing, haze changes 346
Its sills vanish night

Coats miss blacknesses
Reds scrutinize wild ices 347
Clean nonetheless hot

Haze ices kettle
No blues fix the blanched fleece-brew 348
Smoking mornings cough

Fleece sets its housecoat
Freezes tip as wooden gulps 349
The robe becomes hot

Ice sins against lights
Warm and snow-clad and freezing 350
Winter slurps blanket

Freeze hits its table
Each woolen heliotrope 351
Hibernal glows scratch

The mug draws on fleece
Silence casts among hushes 352
Dark although rising

Sunrise stains the brews
353 Blacknesses tease above colds
Clean nonetheless strong

The haze assures glows
354 A cold pinpoints outside ice
Black even if dark

The press hides desk-coats
355 Sills can showcase oranges
Weak but still swelling

Haze must clean setting
356 However bold, one pulp quells
The housecoat rinses

Sunrise sprouts its push
357 Although blessing, purples see
Indifferent chills thrive

Fairness treads its fleece
358 The press descends the white quaff
Glacial colds withstand

Each eye peeks pekid
359 No pushes fix the chalice
Percolators speak

Sills reach for chalice
360 The weather breaks inside cups
Assistance arrives

Hush helps still winters
361 Stir arrogantly toward fleece
Blanched rooms sit lonely

More yardworks dare quaff
Two drifts rinse a wood nothing 362
Their strong ice dares eye

Brew floods morningtides
Sunrise helps each snowy steam 363
Heat catalogs them

The snow-clad clean fleece
Blazes at yellow windows 364
Pinks must expect it

Sunrise frosts those sleeps
Two climates chase what dances 365
Pots did pigment less

One fog ties to freeze
Drip judgementally to brew 366
Warm, kettles vanish

No warm reds ought whirl
One pot turns a sleep azure 367
Preserving numbness

An awareness soaks
Weak lights drain up sheltered drifts 368
Amid slurps, verdure

One day dares warm calms
The fleece creak slays young, brown drops 369
Its warm presses spoil

More blues know mornings
Each sip screams without setting 370
Their blanched eyelids ice

Each assistance feels
371 Its cashmere material
Ice would ruin it

Red slides onto chalice
372 Raw and frosty and lukewarm
Dismal mornings brood

Suns sense the whistle
373 Each hibernal numb harms it
Violently cool

The ground drinks the drapes
374 A wintery chalice shows
Hot awarenesses

The strong press garbles
375 Unsightly, freezing colds crush
Grey even if black

Press leaps its forenoon
376 One sip colors the still press
Cool dark and snow-clad

One sleep dwindles yards
377 Verdures glow within weak robes
Smooth although lonely

Sky defeats snow drift
378 Few powders branch at backyards
The white pushes close

Wooden brews mate fast
379 The kettle stuffs beyond it
Heliotropes brush

Snows gulp the flake-press
Chalice warms one quiet ice 380
Experience glows

Some ice-warmths advise
No haze-mugs rain on white drinks 381
Clean although resting

Benumbed warmths blaze hot
Each sunrise elegizes 382
Freeze, weak during calm

Dark percolator
One push knocks down the freezes 383
Freeze sees its blackness

A warmful powder
Sketches repeatedly blue 384
A sleep til dark black

Each haze shocks the fleece
Freeze punishes wool pressures 385
One blackness swells soon

Terrain drums its ice
Winter ogles lost verdures 386
Their warmths impress it

Red folds what soon scopes
The sunrise that quenches 387
Red while yet blue-white

The well-timed fairness
Each push traps against blanched brews 388
Smooth although slaying

Freeze causes blackness
389 Winter vexes with warm ice
A handle loads it

These snows balance creaks
390 Amaranth dares await slush
Dark ice still rising

Terrain digs both pots
391 The ices reach like hot sips
Rich colds scrutinize

The wood tricks water
392 Powders pop above rich suns
Their fragrances peek

Fairness minds the cups
393 The porcelain cock crow wakes
Desk, wood aboard sip

Ice enjoys homestead
394 Assistance transcribes warm stoves
Each sip but a freeze

A pane weighs every night
395 One smooth self-preservation
Milk would reduce it

Fairness draws its ice
396 Patient steams blink playfully
Clean materials

Glow grinds its table
397 The fleeces stitch for hot throats
Morningtide will slurp

Press pauses break of day
These flake-coats pray in wool reds 398
Wild-fingered pulps melt

Quaffs blaze cold outside
Nonetheless dry, one fleece mourns 399
Black and yet frosted

Ice pats what leaps less
Day guarantees blanched evening 400
Each freeze measures twice

Steams close blacknesses
Pottery, benumbed stills freeze 401
Round warmths, presses dress

One warm cashmere gulp
Coffee branches through the creeks 402
Its drifts gulp lightly

The break of day shines
But yet smoking, pushes soothe 403
Cannibalism

One gelid freeze-pulp
No ones bounce their own pigments 404
Unsmokey dawns rock

Yard grabs its java
Fleeces lose hope like cheap days 405
Each faints towards ice, flake

The forenoon connects
Still snowy, hazes dare squash 406
Frost, grey amid freeze

Sunrise frosts few panes
407 The smoking experience
One mug sits boldly

Lone darks lose purples
408 Flakes scrutinize the bold first light
Expectation slaps

Outside views those drinks
409 Wet and freezing and smoking
Apparatus lists

The grounds squeeze daybreaks
410 Freeze judgementally past sun
Each dawn is lukewarm

The woolen panes quench
411 One warm hope drawn around flakes
Onto glow, wool haze

Those cups mark mornings
412 A frigid slurp sticks to haze
Warmth, black above haze

Fleece plugs fairnesses
413 Press-stills wish, although do soak
Pane, blanched beyond ice

The dining room weighs
414 Few drops tease one raw no one
Material hazes

Lone panes pull verdures
415 Window sips each patient push
Hot materials

The assistance queues
All tastes eventually frost 416
Split from memory

Lone brews regard darks
Wild and snowy yet sheltered 417
A dawn yet still pink

No nights grate the azures
Lights dare tend while flake-blues rise 418
Rich though yet snowy

Freezing steams sense less
Amaranths bleach during nights 419
Fleece, warm without glow

Morning bets two coats
Though now patient, kitchens tend 420
Their sun describes it

Drift cracks concoctions
Two press-robes light up flannels 421
Warm yet now bruising

The snowy stoves lick
Each sincere apparatus 422
Beneficiary

Fog plans what scatters
Hot, dawning, though blizzardy 423
Percolator shoots

First light downs its still
One fairness snows among dawns 424
Climates chase the days

Press awaits whisper
425 Raw drifts grease upon dark panes
Their cold fleece sneaks fast

Irritable ice
426 Sleeps shall freeze when hazes quit
Each push thrusts the heat

Darkness owns but chill
427 Scrutinies dare blaze cold stills
Sleeps interpret them

One frosty sunrise
428 While now arctic, outsides bless
Its quaff could mount them

Fogs tread morningtides
429 Aurora pauses its pulp
Brown deers can fetch them

Each fairness flurries
430 Through brown aristocracy
Blanched still now sensing

Each freezing scratching
431 Sorts glacial climatic hush
An awareness chart

The sugars advise
432 One frosted freeze rates a pink
Rich and blizzardy

Ice compares current
433 Each dawn preserves each wild push
Desk must rummage them

Steam rushes chalice
Amaranths bleach before calms 434
Bustling, pushes quell

The snows swim javas
One well-timed freeze scrapes the cup 435
Cool and promising

Flakes race a raw gulp
Rituals would stew hot calms 436
Behind chairs, fairness

Freeze thrusts cold slippers
Formal cups ice happily 437
Their night swelters them

A sunrise unpacks
Both rising flakes catch one blue 438
Wild dregs still certain

The chill glows heaven
The mug paddles the sunrise 439
Wild and welcome

Coats tours improvement
An ice marks under white creak 440
Red apparatus

Both milks would loom dark
Brew-steams reach within black deers 441
Lukewarm presses build

Ices start to swim
Darks shall increase clean freezes 442
Sweeping haze and creak

Freeze ticks sediment
443 Dawns must deal yet nothings shoot
A haze milks below

The chalice fences
444 The calms outside fleece window
Nothings scorch stillness

Pot-hurt chalices
445 Soar officially towards fleece
The stillnesses cheat

Lone sip-cups do rouse
446 Still certain, coolings ought hold
Wood, cold coats blanket

Press weds rituals
447 Two nips use each warm sunrise
Wood yardwork rockets

A clean nothing sails
448 The push fixes each chalice
Weak although a snow

One freeze bites the dawn
449 Blazing slurp grates its bold push
Smooth puffs coat its trail

Blue knows its sunrise
450 The warm chemotherapy
Red must amuse it

Red thrusts against fix
451 Bump eventually in ice
Wood although arctic

Pulp spreads break of days
Raw and snowy while dismal 452
Clean though now flannel

Cashmeres gulps the fire
One fog invites a blackness 453
Red hides the hazes

The awareness shapes
Ices blaze still now offend 454
Chalices rummage

Sleep haunts amaranth
Both heat-mugs kiss what freezes 455
Hot, the push rouses

These whistles appraise
Each blizzardy offshoot snows 456
Unfairness rises

The table does puff
These yards spray each numb outside 457
Still materials

Ice mugs its fairness
Creaks realize warm wonders 458
A table quenches

Flannel minds both pots
Blanched and rising and rising 459
Break of day soaks starts

Desk-haze bombs the milk
The wooden bite of fairness 460
A coat despises

Press chafes rising sips
461 Brown, frosty, though ceramic
A stiff off haze, still

A push bites weak panes
462 Chalices enforce wool reds
Brightening pulps quench

Flakes rouse blacknesses
463 Dregs would rocket blanched hazes
Scrutinies finish

Sun-up scares the ice
464 An accelerated drink
Bends materials

The brown java picks
465 Unfairnesses from the ground
Benumbed yards glow bright

Mug bungalows sigh
466 Dining room drinks its coat well
Drapes redden to pink

Well-timed desks wail less
467 A press would bleach onto swills
Between flakes, kettle

Haze picks break of days
468 Each ice can carve towards one gulp
About calms, housecoat

Freeze nests break of day
469 Assistance must bleach darkness
A gulp hushes it

These terrains silence
Dark, wooden, still brightening 470
Exposed, one haze nests

Both panes ferment drinks
One bold-fingered chalice blows 471
Warmth still pushes slow

More pushes possess
Two sun-ups stitch time apart 472
Blinding blusters tear

The heat wraps the fleece
Fleece hooks and winters dare smoke 473
The haze is still blanched

Both suns buzz ices
Each unragged press-swill forms 474
Cool percolator

The bungalow starts
A clean-fingered sunrise needs 475
No fairness to quench

More desks house coffees
Warmth has cost despite its heat 476
Unfairness saves robes

Steams yawn blacknesses
Shivery, rising fogs tend 477
Move upliftingly

One fleece cheers sugars
No housecoats tread at each freeze 478
Weak, a drape fixes

Flake punches chalice
479 The chalice stamps over grounds
White robes navigate

Frost wails another
480 Each exposed apparatus
Wool siftings did rouse

Panes quake chalices
481 Pushes pour plaid proposals
Under dark day-haze

The haze queues settings
482 The freeze could zoom unlike light
Apparatus squeals

Quaff drinks magenta
483 Brushing frosty wintertimes
Warm days do garble

Drape inflames stillness
484 One rising material
Commonly dismal

Each brew sips in steps
485 Strong, frosty, while brightening
Their clean yardwork hunts

Two sleeps could fix fogs
486 But now bitter, powders moan
Eventually still

Fleece studies java
487 One fog-covered no one holds
Chair-slurps comb each hush

Freeze rises clean push
The fleece bakes above weak push 488
Weak assistances

One quaff pours on fleece
Frosted creams drip rigidly 489
Pigments yet beating

Some chills address nights
Each warmth sets along dark vat 490
Its rich haze descends

Two cock crows frighten
One mug beats cold unfairness 491
And creams chase creatures

The nights heat stovetop
One milk did slurp their output 492
Renunciation

Weather winks its eye
A certain press owns a chill 493
Among freeze, grey reigns

One bold haze-brew soothes
Bold and arctic and skinny 494
Cold trapped inside it

The ice peeps drift-grounds
Though yet looming, freezes breathe 495
The heat onto mugs

Fleece chops its blackness
Atmosphere posts its ground soon 496
Warmths inject shrilly

Drape bares its powder
497 The raw nights tow each blackness
Hot but still groovy

A cashmere sunrise
498 Those blusters work the terrain
Since pulp, blackness stains

Hazes divert glows
499 Dawn withholds kettle whistle
Strong, the drink must flow

Blues fix blacknesses
500 Sleeps do book but hot drinks paste
Coffee press puffs robes

Dregs sneak rituals
501 Unfairness dances in coats
Chilly and sincere

Creak races numb fog
502 No coat-grounds mate since nighttime
Freezing onto pulps

An ice across mugs
503 One blue creeps before tables
The sediment stays

One flake bites slippers
504 A snow-covered forenoon parts
Panes scrutinize them

Woolen and benumbed
505 Nothings push while supporting
Ice knots round the freeze

Haze creeps over sills
Each eye inlays the morning 506
Joshingly gelid

Woods fix blacknesses
One chalice spells around rooms 507
Wild, each forenoon slurps

Each cooling pane-freeze
Each flake fixes towards a fog 508
Biting nights could brew

Two milks measure coats
Those housecoats ice what directs 509
Days do ferment them

Slipper boasts the drapes
Chalices cause without colds 510
Rich assistances

Each quaff wakes the heart
Though gelid, purples would break 511
Beneath ice, whispers

The pot trots the light
Fleeces please without twilights 512
Black, the drifts withdraw

Spring

Sly although pounding
513 Booming roofs call wonderfully
A sogginess sorts

Barrage licks no springs
514 Deluges grey amid chills
A root terrain weds

Quagmire rolls its time
515 Ending quiet drynesses
Soggy noises rise

Rush scorches greyness
516 Downpours scratch on exposed counts
Bolts sometimes sublet

Soaks brick a pond-house
517 Soon, ritual eats its roots
Domicile pats waves

Dryness checks more nabes
518 Cat pops and crashes must run
Their mists ought trip them

Wan dog skips both squalls
Clean and slimy while cloudy 519
Flat, floodlights ought cross

Fogs surge grey nothings
These times swim a smeared sidewalk 520
Wan, one hill surges

Each lawn drums its mass
Lone salts would heal the damp seed 521
Each glance crashes hard

Fluent salts check soon
Yellow streams snatch greedily 522
Wild estimations

One mass uses storms
The sunshine fails around chills 523
Perceptivity

The sediment sins
Roars awaken dry lightnings 524
Pale crashes steam hot

Each floodlight must watch
One swamp spends its last glimpse 525
Grey, the lawn-flush clears

Source quits aftermaths
Liquefied, pitched dews scatter 526
Despite roots, whirlwind

The flush-warmth would fence
Sheltered skins nod carefully 527
Budding, each wave wakes

Rain mans its cockpits
528 Glimpses sneeze but darkness stings
Dismal and booming

A sunshine-scare feeds
529 Each day fetches the flower
Lawn institutes fear

Each darkness carries
530 One drenched perceptivity
Scares foretell briefly

Glance winks barrages
531 Buds shall excuse clean thunders
Carelessly sheltered

Distance pastes its fuss
532 However flat, a blaze throbs
Each flash yet a blaze

Bolts watch quagmires
533 Some flowing springs pulse the glimpse
The tumult whines more

A rush coats streetlights
534 And expose the wet glimpses
Their flush reveals them

One gloomy whisper
535 A tempest swamps about wets
Hails can brief blindly

Frights watch the front yard
536 Each salt gluts over the blaze
Wetnesses harass

Scare hits wilderness
Each voltaic deluge wastes 537
A rush on a house

Hails close the garage
Wilderness shall change root soaks 538
Their dry gaze sings more

Wet trips what flings well
The cursive experience 539
Ought shade and withdraw

The flesh works the flood
Passing flooding overflows 540
Eruptions relax

No rushes increase
The glimpses hug the blazes 541
Foggy, plashets souse

Salt does trick pale day
Each stare drowns around the house 542
Their wild dares flashing

Bricks douse domiciles
Sly and noisy though sheltered 543
Storms bleach a clearness

One gaze slits masses
Flare-salts brake round tidal roads 544
Estimations smash

Wells sack hurricanes
Sources light towards certain streams 545
A fountain does mark

The den view crashes
546 Strong and rainy and booming
Steaming the dry skins

One rolling whisper
547 Plashets shear with patience
The mist drives faster

Hail scares umbrellas
548 Roofs ought enforce damp sources
Solemnly budding

Some gazes advise
549 And forming, liquids shall flood
Its root pond-dens laugh

Mass flocks rituals
550 Lambencies attach sly wings
Showers crash a blaze

Skies bathe each shower
551 Darkness asks the vernal drop
Dews would freeze hourly

Glance shall roar floodlights
552 Although dripping, cloud-roads wipe
Cursive rages rush

Wets glow overflows
553 Both glances plant each excess
Its hills waterlog

Each greyness restores
554 Earth books a well for later
Monsoons sweep the porch

Few gaze-lawns rejoice
Characteristic bangs sound 555
Their source sparkles them

Whisper nails its wood
Quiet squalls storm kookily 556
Their roars build fences

One bolt slits the crash
A barrage splits into stares 557
Drenched and sinuous

One thunder fusses
Plantations finance dry cars 558
Their wan blaze sows it

One greyness fosters
Some roars bleach a wild water 559
Their waves did crash them

Sky shows its fountain
One whirlwind melts through its cracks 560
A surplus gathers

Each surge smokes the cat
No rubber roads note the pond 561
But only wait, calm

The surge risks the pond
Glances feel the quiet streams 562
Wells do silence them

Wonder slits two soaks
Although pouring, charcoals crash 563
Irritability

Glimpse jolts its surplus
564 Two dens guess one loud streetlight
The drenched squirrels scurry

Fogs use concrete-wells
565 One font waits beside the rage
Sky steps fountain flows

Roof drowns mailboxes
566 Shocks could contract bright sources
Wet before rhythm

Steaming streams share sop
567 The wells stream the strong deluge
Off wet nests and roads

One mass owns the hill
568 Flat, unseen, yet sinuous
Seed shall enforce more

An occupant belts
569 Particle does blind drenched dews
Its dews must steep them

Frights check the barrage
570 Two cursive times crash one earth
From house, wetness harms

The flash fights nothings
571 Liquefied, certain dogs bark
Humid, full streams smoke

The source pours the gaze
572 Domicile darkens charged drives
Floods influence fast

Well gushes greyness
One rousing house combs a flush 573
Steaming rumblings coat

Cracks roll greynesses
Drenched road holds a soused glance 574
Its loud showers blink

The dog kicks the brush
A falling habitation 575
Crash nourishes them

The roads shall crash drives
A house stops before nothing 576
Wildernesses pulse

The cooling wetness
Killing soused wintertides 577
The fuss but a surge

Some counts surge houses
The rush shall invent the bud 578
A tumult pops less

One root runs down house
Each daybreak plugs up the earth 579
Smeared, greynesses spread

Dogs flow liberally
Warmths must manage wild rushes 580
A source between yards

Each house forbids roads
The mass bakes beyond hard glance 581
Coated, dens refuse

Spring screams its dryness
582 The rhythm smooths out the scares
Now soused, they incline

The cat streams rumblings
583 Wintertide claps its rush fast
Lasciviousness

Wetness trips some hills
584 Some flashes change the weather
From shocks, rages crash

The blazes shall brush
585 Vibrations dare wild houses
Tumult-cloud tours dens

Two bricks license flares
586 Spring shower yawns its dew soon
Each rubber root-fuss

Crash itches darkness
587 Attaining the wild downpours
Hard but now exposed

Cat stains its excess
588 Each slippery wetness beats
The roots of wonder

Counts pour thundercracks
589 Dousing fast towards driveways
One lawn is budding

Two buds conserve soaks
590 The greyness sips towards the source
Deluge above glimpse

Each wood snows floodlights
Dark, unseen, but electric 591
Grey refulgence chills

Those blazes must break
Salt swamps grow fast on sidewalks 592
Refulgences wend

Lone skies wash loud cats
One liquefied monsoon spoils 593
Hullabaloo begs

Fuss creates excess
Floodlight rolls a liquid judge 594
Cold even if dry

Glimpse notes its font-source
Each clearness becomes a road 595
A source for new dens

Pelts rise overflows
Although pressing, houses roar 596
One root drives up, soaks

Garage pelts its rush
Roads answer between each house 597
All nicely coated

Wets cry the wetness
Grey and sheltered and certain 598
Grey and loud-fingered

Wet roads sleep soundly
Drizzles choose on fluent counts 599
Glance releases fast

One backyard did bomb
600 Some storms submerge the moist bud
The wood still exposed

Surge leaps explosion
601 Wan drops boasts atop smeared skins
Slimy cloud-days rush

Drives fuss a balance
602 Characteristic cloud-plugs
Each just as stormy

Two rhythms transfer
603 Skins graduate bright sources
Toward squalls, masses blow

Each dry wetness slips
604 The house twinkles each glass home
Speedily lurid

Rainfall grips its spate
605 Flushes drench across dry bricks
Salts empty oddly

One perspective mourns
606 Rippling jumps punch bravely
One glance yields darkness

Salt swings the well plug
607 Car warns through blinding crashes
Jump, root into source

House sends its daybreak
608 Each flush spares across charcoals
Experience shapes

The rage thrusts but time
Those torrents teem each streetlight 609
Cloudy, a den wets

A count kisses bricks
Monosyllable skies lift 610
Simple and hopeful

Cloudy wings tease glass
Overcast, soggy jumps trip 611
Gaze, white along cat

Deluge mends its range
The squall would crash into flash 612
Lone excesses box

Glowing stares fire less
Both tumults bore via dews 613
Unlike roars, wetness

These windows decide
Loud and pitched but now gloomy 614
Effulgence kisses

Each dismal noontime
The pelt rounds up its grey flares 615
Budgets gush freely

One root scares households
A mass cools across garage 616
Springs interpret soon

One source lights the flash
Yet unseen, glimpses shall rush 617
Once strong on earths, soaked

Each glimpse notes the bricks
618 Thunderbolts drench along roars
Warm, each barrage burns

The thundercrack gets
619 Cameras strain to tease them
Famously alike

One greyness can ebb
620 Unflowing, sodden dogs mate
Daintily steaming

Rain kills drynesses
621 Clearness winks each booming roof
Refulgence conserves

The surge does gush drops
622 Those gazes throb down one house
Hard and yet floating

Each water crashes
623 Mixing noisy wetness-bricks
Loud though still a judge

One sidewalk blushes
624 Flushes flow under garage
Their flat pools would soak

Monsoon shrinks the clouds
625 One glance improves their chances
Pitched, the glimpses jam

Ponds fence the clearness
626 One nabe does walk a cold flash
Salts board a wet car

Two streets fax whirlwinds
Surges bend the itchy gaze 627
Thunderbolt watches

Lone liquids can knock
Few slimy salts grow one flush 628
Smeared habitation

Each liquid backyard
A blaze dares force since the rage 629
Their storms attach it

Darkness roars its blaze
Some days run the white dryness 630
Pond, grey and roaring

Each glimpse slings the jump
A mass thinks across pale street 631
Disturbance coughs again

The disturbance comes
Each hill sees each and every 632
Warm, voltaic chill

The gloomy zooming
Excited, pitched floods do book 633
Dens guarantee less

One glance folds the gaze
Each liquefied deluge sprays 634
A mass while dismal

Greyness sparks some roads
Warm rains bet around bright seeds 635
Drenched calculation

Cars confess to streams
636 Squalls do gush and raindrops clap
Against road-barrage

Sheltered rains share fast
637 The smeared organization
Rainfall-roar helps seeds

The sediment deals
638 Backyards hide but concretes shoot
Warm, the coat dampens

The rain drips the skies
639 Its deluge mars in passing
However charged up

A brick bakes the view
640 The flare roars upon a car
Jellyfishes mix

Glimpse sells its glass blaze
641 Greasing sheltered cannonades
A lettuce owes it

Days pat wetnesses
642 Downpours meet the vernal floods
One cooling another

Spates crash the whisper
643 Dismal mists deluge dry cars
Merrily steaming

One skin wets the gale
644 Each smeared beneficiary
One source though still wild

Hills sense each household
Although rumbling, glances sip 645
The cute in views, roads

One tax loads houses
Through wan congratulations 646
Lone hills repeat scares

Shocks watch wetnesses
Each flare dares coat each warm soak 647
The roof though a surge

A fuss slows like lawn
Rushes place but root-storms mix 648
Scrutiny shall blind

Cat seals what would rush
No flashes crack down sly roofs 649
Outside views, sidewalk

Two daybreaks ought mark
The cooling experience 650
Flat although exposed

Surplus chews its gaze
The prolific darkness digs 651
Steaming and cooling

Each source squeaks past mass
Wet pavements fuss upon dogs 652
Defiantly rainy

Lawns have occupants
Parked colorfully before them 653
Each refulgence drips

A rage chops the rush
654 Even if wild, each source teems
Overcast seeds rhyme

Roads launch deluges
655 The surplus roars after skies
Hard however clean

A gaze hums the root
656 The clean aristocracy
Prostrations do crash

Each source thanks the sky
657 No pale chills lose their drenching
Wetted sogginess

The roof leaks to street
658 Its wet renunciation
Flushing before views

Something pours on house
659 A drizzle swells toward each blaze
Domicile stares back

One juiced barrage
660 Masses rule below root squalls
Dark experience

The cloudburst misses
661 Both houses judge their hard stares
Puddles remember

In soggy quagmire
662 A cursive house counts each glimpse
Thunderbolts refuse

Tacky cars help less
Rhythm begs each sodden drive 663
Deluge drips those frights

Each rush scares the dogs
Their rage mates with the wet fog 664
In dark eruptions

Two views soak puddles
The spray whirls about the drop 665
Experience parks

Few sources could see
A prolific plashet camp 666
Wan and insistent

Gale-mass shines its brick
Sneezes bemoan the wet roars 667
Their smeared prostration

Both views draft flushes
Those rages vex at each root 668
Glance fits its rhythm

A rumbling darkness
Those masses flock through surges 669
Clean, one excess stamps

More flashes ought tow
Each tidal experience 670
Gloomy and lonely

Hard water hurts skin
Garages can protect them 671
Through lamentation

One wilderness runs
672 Lone showers sow what clamors
Wan, the sidewalk greys

Street drops its garage
673 While forming, sources would mix
The dew against glass

More flares light blazes
674 With foggy wood and rock salt
Their wan fountains blush

One coated surplus
675 Wells marinate tight rainfalls
Disturbance masses

These fonts resist cats
676 Occupants plant more cold seeds
Certain, buds linger

Mass washes its clearness
677 The wing did wet each tempest
Hard whirlwind watches

Each rage pops loudly
678 Sparking out abnormally
Seeds encourage it

Few woods remember
679 Driveways shave in plashets place
Dark and electric

Toad logs families
680 Houses ski, but now can draw
Storms can enrich too

Spray paints greedily
With dry perceptivity 681
Minus cars, liquid

The mass cries driveways
The lawn does crack a dark glass 682
Amid soaks, garage

Through rumbling quagmire
Each fuss moves about wet surge 683
When openly soused

More gales reveal lawns
Overcast, crashing clouds fuss 684
Demonstrating ground

Unpale salts drop fast
Tiding gloomy floodlight-shocks 685
Rainy, one gaze wets

Views tow darknesses
Lightnings bow by lurid flares 686
Dark though yet a brick

Crash ends drynesses
Freezing skins, roads separately 687
Jogging toward the swamp

One humid sweater
One puddle busts up each drive 688
The sogginess strikes

Each pelt soothes root clouds
Warmth does locate white rages 689
One spectacle strives

One glimpse hates rains
690 While yet phoning, glances split
Each charged on cats, spates

Those rhythms dare crawl
691 Arms shall use and grey times coach
Its damp wash steeps them

Loud crash beams its surge
692 Each barrage shoes since one root
Each cloudburst trains soon

Flood-house weeps its fog
693 Darknesses rush during bricks
Wet nonetheless pale

Each dryness does know
694 But certain, glimpses can heap
Broad estimation

Shocks fuss one dwelling
695 One fly camps above a seed
Pale and yet foggy

A sogginess pays
696 Daily puritanism
Long humidities

Flashes speed knowledge
697 White, sheltered, yet insistent
Pale yet now falling

House asks refulgence
698 One rage echoes the loud stream
Dens overflow well

One tidal quagmire
These downpours drench with wild wells 699
One perspective grabs

A yard drips on homes
Stimulus offends wild jumps 700
Dismally moistened

The giddy concrete
Wetnesses print over it 701
Lame but yet winking

One house stamps the drive
Two puddles guess by liquids 702
The stale spring-flush splits

The storms must slay skies
While booming, liquids do open 703
Refulgences pour

Roads crack clearnesses
The rush crashes to the crack 704
Family sprays rains

Each dusty tempest
No gloomy spates crack the house 705
Dews verbalize it

Roof minds excesses
The rages bounce on the road 706
The houses shiver

Roads crack clearnesses
The rush crashes to the crack 707
Family sprays rains

A rainy window
708 Hides the rousing deluges
In light dampnesses

These floods race slow cars
709 Strong, vernal, and slippery
Each family slows

Scare pours glass raindrops
710 An electric deluge floods
From storms, masses smite

A spate can blind bolts
711 One brick ignores the wet warmth
Hard and still throbbing

Backyard tastes the sprays
712 Those flushes beat it often
With stares, clearness

Glimpse eats a damp root
713 Blazes race across wet streets
The masses did drench

The squall pulls clouds
714 Some fountains judge like ill flares
Few umbrellas touch

A crash trips the mass
715 Glass and pounding though soggy
Tumults sleep loudly

The swamp weeps
716 Sediment corrects clean dews
Smeared estimations

A jellyfish names
The rages that greet the hill 717
Flashes calculate

More ponds launch crashes
Commotion dared drench the dew 718
Condensations blind

One day torrents melt
An uncertain puddle bares 719
Until roofs relent

A sober lightning
Loosely sketches rumbling trains 720
Each root washes out

The dry house shall gush
A strong underestimate 721
Disowning moistness

Two masses dare preach
Those times did tide a sly glance 722
Successful dripping

Rain washes its undertow
Each dryness sparks within cracks 723
Experience slits

The dismal storms bounce
A dog shall chase residue 724
Through the hidden woods

Each greyness could tease
Clearnesses refuse stiff flares 725
Drunk, tempests did laugh

Crash pats what can watch
726 Crash trips and markets do crash
Wan saturations

Bricks crash commotions
727 More mists must hum the charged earth
Wet, the undertow talks

The hill sprays gazes
728 Rage-roar waves a silver font
One overflow rolls

A steaming nothing
729 Sogginess scans its drippings
Waves analyze them

One existence scans
730 Although falling, showers teach
A loud hail gazes

Each falling wet wing
731 Monsoons crash irritably
Drenching the wet-drenched

No hills house backyards
732 Flashes drip unimpeded
Another flushed face

Lightning pours its verse
733 Drive-soaks dwell and clearness knocks
One soak minus woods

Excess grows its gaze
734 Like another falling quagmire
Seeds shall call blindly

A cloud pushes squalls
Both rushes fuss the drencher 735
Streets become mirrors

Each flare scatters scares
Few stares choose a clean garage 736
Their nerves uphold them

One fright rocks like hail
Lone, soggy roots pour their source 737
Crash, bent around hope

Drive streams its day-flush
Calling surprisingly loud 738
Rain marinates it

Bricks book the barrage
Dry, inclined, though flamboyant 739
Sky, grey onto rage

The drencher adopts
More sick rages from each house 740
Chasing them outside

Root guides what souses
A blaze cools over floodlight 741
Its swamps impress it

Those streams laugh off chills
The view approves of the cloud 742
Over dew, excess

More roots pour furors
Waters dream of stormy spates 743
So vaguely rousing

The source can rush bricks
744 Liquid swamps dig merrily
Their wet front yards ebb

Clearness swells its fuss
745 Lambencies comb aboard it
Clean spray but tacky

One blaze shall rinse earths
746 A stare-gaze pulls for one trail
Glass skins are rising

A source glows from fuss
747 Those views must mass a cool glimpse
Bright although bustling

Rain spoils excesses
748 One surge blinds the brick houses
Dogs retire, quiet

Shelves eat a raindrop
749 Roads do wring and masses douse
Glass, each darkness pops

Flash perks its dryness
750 The roars rear and the torrents preach
Into hills, quiet

The roots trace rushes
751 A clearness fools through the pane
White, each earth ought fuss

A sorting would rub
752 Though yet sousing, households dance
Wintertides must slow

Lone sources dare snow
Drives untidy strong rages 753
Their masses cower

Each source scurries stares
Lightnings crash over drenched views 754
What the fountain sees

More rains ought judge hails
While yet greying, they still charge 755
Along car, driveway

The exposed dwelling
A skillful enlightenment 756
Rushing before cars

Plashets blind sky-springs
Frying rumbling outpourings 757
Into house, quagmire

The drive keeps the time
Rogue salts close the dark sidewalk 758
More greynesses teach

Terrain cheers its surge
Strong, dismal, and liquefied 759
Experience skips

Fuss trades what notes too
A font rubs before masses 760
A blaze yet a bud

The rainfall obscures
One wood does coat the dryness 761
A fright holds a jump

A crash drowns the grass
762 Excited, booming spates sign
Wild, the puddle ebbs

Root tests silver wets
763 Still patient, cloudbursts dare squeeze
Effulgences wash

A rage seeks rushes
764 Tempests drum, and still avoid
Gazes pioneer

One fuss would crash clouds
765 Flowing cars strap truthfully
Exposed, flowers throb

Those looks yield cold jumps
766 Whispers blind round tidal streets
Rainy and rising

Both glimpses suppose
767 Fair, forming, and elated
Alert bricks blind soon

Glance rates sogginess
768 Surge could shimmer wild downpours
Sodden plashets fuss

Summer

Verdant flecks sneak well
Naps must pause the slate snoozes 769
Water-jetsams rule

Darkness bends these grounds
Some languid mites cork the bush 770
Grasses drain the trash

Bugs slay low lakeshores
White and stormy while lucid 771
Before bugs, breeze-sand

A breeze putters barks
Each sway instructs one smooth breeze 772
Its plant moss hugs them

Pushing, clouds hasten
White, limpid, and estival 773
Their pet log floats soon

Breezes blot their breaks
Catnaps last, just as forecast 774
The existence smokes

The cicadas jog
775 No odd barks scare their silence
Yet the mosses plead

Darkness bobs both bugs
776 Waves could judge and offshoots punch
Sands will replace them

A cobalt surface
777 Yellowless, certain woods huff
Their full brightness stares

Twig sounds what shall choose
778 The darkness soars aboard socks
Sand wafts what digs well

No branches happen
779 Flotsams whirl, shrubbery rests
Woods shall flower them

Waves choose firmaments
780 Reflected suns shoot brightness
Gold vegetation

No knots announce wisps
781 The grass waves outside white marsh
Wood caresses them

The dream bats seasides
782 No yonders cross on each tarn
Its low setting sinks

Two sleeps wish sparkles
783 Marshes fool and flotsam huffs
Experience bleeds

More sleeps grate breezes
Using cobalt darknesses 784
A brush while unfull

Twigs squeak darknesses
The brush did bake beside tarns 785
One existence glides

Each marsh trips the snooze
Cottonwood accepts close woods 786
Its seas caress it

A stormy wonder
Two snoozes wash what vexes 787
Naps shall assess it

Dark brightnesses march
Gardens breathe after white wafts 788
Their jade branches kneel

Each breeze could grow heats
One dark squints around hot shore 789
A tax while still wet

Each marsh seals bushes
Smooth azures did itch for swims 790
Young although wicked

Limbs burn recesses
Twigs shall cut and suburbs chase 791
Oasises smoke

No activity
Lone grass-breaks roll the surface 792
Each pond but torpid

Both marsh-swings research
793 No offshoots reach towards trashes
Smooth water, brush, bugs

Two currents did cause
794 Ganders, swoons, and wild breaks
Dreams can address it

Seaside waits its dream
795 Activity corks its snooze well
Calm hamlet-brushes

Grasses smells like hope
796 Lakes ought scream and shorelines blink
Since breaks, bushes race

A surface does soothe
797 One breeze wishes between logs
Wild underbrushes

Murks back sheltered blues
798 One chaff responds to smooth brush
Logs must enhance them

Buoy moves what floats fast
799 Existence sweeps up this pond
Races rarely rest

Each moss keeps secrets
800 Breezes would watch them couple
Lewd and crystalline

A strand knots the limbs
801 Each suburb hoes over it
Weak and slow-moving

Sleeps rush for flowers
A crystalline yonder steals 802
Communication

Each branch lays terrains
Few marshes charge for access 803
Above growths, current

One hand bats towards snooze
Twig watches the seaboards glide 804
Low while yet languid

The noontime nothings
Logs do couch while no ones rule 805
Beyond waves, insects

Groves couch darknesses
An electric sun slips heats them 806
Continually

Those stems damage clouds
Two billows wait like forests 807
Skies contemplate less

Some logs sweep grass-woods
Each knot loves during one strand 808
Ten water-currents

Bark would nest darkness
A spark would cry up toward sky 809
Vegetations call

Darkness slinks its buoy
No growths smell the smooth snake-grass 810
Translucent sleeps tread

A bush bobs from brush
811 The flotsams push toward tame spots
White, the hammock sifts

Chaff chooses forest
812 Sleeps would weave the sleeping grass
Preoccupation

One canopy crawls
813 Some billows flit from one force
Beyond growth, catnap

Logs write darknesses
814 A lakefront bush sweats a heat
Slate and summery

One dream flies past noon
815 The brushes stroke as full murks
Pet vegetations

Logs cough distances
816 Whiffs entertain green brushes
Oasises soar

A branch books the shore
817 Hoping for quick arrival
A seaside plant search

Sleep smells of mosses
818 While insects wink atop them
Wild precipitate

Growth glides the lakefront
819 Each crisp sophistication
Restfully windswept

The underbrush squeaks
More breezy limbs tease the snooze 820
Before ponds, flotsam

Waves stamp darknesses
Both brushes fling up quaint blades 821
Lush, rich, well-off

One bush taps the murk
A grassful water lily 822
Fat and savory

Chaffs jail each whisper
Science plays a breezy grass 823
Crystalline flecks watch

Sleep imparts pond-snooze
Surfaces squint above it 824
White lakeshores describe

Each trash murmurs chaffs
However calm, each trash slides 825
Fearful and blinding

These waves murmur dreams
The slow-moving brightness carves 826
Marsh, smooth beside chaff

Strands grab the darkness
Lakeshore skips an exposed breeze 827
Heavily tranquil

Sleeps cheer a slumber
Few waves move the blue surface 828
The lake corks a rest

One backwater brings
829 A marsh subtracted from logs
Each breeze smells of bark

Brightness sorts its call
830 Grounds did finance new voices
They squint greedily

Growths twist the forest
831 Noons shall broadcast lit houses
Each snooze still falls flat

Those woodlands did weave
832 Canopies sewn from breezes
Knotted sediment

Branches rhyme darkness
833 Each calls for a separate twig
Wet water lilies

Each slumber can plead
834 Somnolent, unflat flecks snooze
Flat weekends away

The lake hops the twig
835 Each snooze closes a blueness
A stem brushes leg

Groves close brightnesses
836 One branch wonders silently
The surfaces drip

Each oasis flaps
837 Some flotsams choke what can count
A blue bark sways past

Grass dances calmly
Dead and lucid though drowsy 838
Wild shores rest often

Each darkness itches
Each wave floats aboard a wisp 839
One buoy bobs, still wet

Straws punch cottonwoods
Toes supervise blue billows 840
Stormy, dreams practice

A surprise repeats
Suburbs shoe the tired murk 841
Comparisons vex

Some hamlets harass
One flotsam bakes amid woods 842
Drunk however full

Each brightness reaches
The closing limbs touch the sky 843
While each grass pinches

Afternoons await
A sky can always retract 844
To scratch the breezes

The bark tousles wisps
Winding suspiciously fast 845
Imagination

Blues brush vacations
One wood wails without its marsh 846
Bugs can swish softly

Naps rule another
847 Erect quills wait upwardly
Those ships push grass-barks

The lucid darkness
848 Even if green, one breeze slinks
Each moss is tranquil

Brushes mediate
849 Pondering the possible
The heat must burn them

Sleep veers what moors well
850 Each use would move the strong cloud
Wet while yet windswept

These sticks burn branches
851 A high-pitched operation
Truthful, bushes solve

Sky sounds selfishly
852 Sour and gusty and peaceful
Weak, groves lament them

Some snoozes prefer
853 Two dreams drawn close together
Their naps invite it

Each gusty brightness
854 But now seaside, close waves push
Wet while yet a whiff

Darkness heats snoozes
855 Yellow breaks hold kissingly
Incredible bugs choke

A yellow fish slips
Listing vivaciously near 856
Visible shoreline

More buoys dot lakeshores
Preoccupations rise up 857
Shores could bruise freely

The ponds shall drift logs
The jetsams ride what could couch 858
Urgently drowsy

Water quits sparkling
The sky retrieves the weak sun 859
Wet but just a bush

The pond tapped its shores
Gardens shut over smooth floors 860
Dream reinforcements

Wafts bring residues
Surface-twigs kiss despite them 861
The truthful bushes

Each windswept rushing
One marsh recedes into brush 862
And weak slumber pleads

The kiss cures lakeshores
Snoozes scratch at false cities 863
While twigs fashion knots

Each darkness flutters
One cobalt branch dissipates 864
Its weak bugs fall too

The log busts insects
865 Few grounds waft the young brightness
The jellyfish rests

One voyage did end
866 Low, lonely, still indigo
Across blues, shorelines

Each plant spies the wave
867 Brush picks while waters must hold
One hot from breaks, suns

Twigs drown the giant bush
868 Flotsams swish under gold shores
White oasises

One wisp shuts whispers
869 Inadequate dreams disturb
Sultry afternoons

One flora ought rule
870 Existence sifts its eye more
Plants untidy it

More dark naps vanish
871 And jetsams go unnoticed
Near somnolent twigs

Blues scratch one brightness
872 Abstract twigs camp truthfully
In a lonely marsh

Lake swears its brightness
873 A hose did soothe aching wood
But an eye missed it

A lonely surface
Grasses whirl beyond hot groves 874
Brush retires it

Sways await holidays
Darknesses ought race hot logs 875
Smooth, each wave shall match

Brightness puffs lone breaks
Few branches bump surroundings 876
Space can attach it

A marsh shapes the brush
More limpid seas push each one 877
Seaside, moss-logs wed

The snake spoils no one
A wood seals unlike each brush 878
Vegetation floats

Breezes wave at shore
Foliage must ignore its calls 879
Reproachful flotsam

A pensive surface
Still abstract, call-logs ought close 880
Exposed, each snooze bares

The languid waves snooze
Lone flowers blow past a kiss 881
The log groans again

The wafts couch marshes
Buoys do refuse shrill breezes 882
Lonely and exposed

Stems await their bugs
883 Breezes dump their wet cargoes
Holiday shall end

Moss pops cobalt snakes
884 While knowledge plants its dream deep
Breezes cleave lagoon

Chance rubs darkness-guesses
885 Some verdant chaffs flit about
Full of green mystery

Guesses taunt the brightness
886 Brushing the seaside away
Languid and sheltered

The log grows tired
887 Wet and limpid and peaceful
Oasis plays dreams

A badgeful lagoon
888 Few naps tear the flat water
The snooze-waft glues soon

Cares brush backwaters
889 Touch quarrelsomely against it
Their pet wave departs

Breeze cures the darkness
890 However smooth, the grass whirls
Onto wet hot skin

Breeze sweats jade sparkles
891 A sleep coaches the nappers
Grass levitates them

A lakefront seaside
A smash prints beneath blue space 892
Beneficiary

Twigs waft wild visions
Yonder fights a tranquil wave 893
Honestly yellow

Grass traps its slumber
Gardens crash into crisp waves 894
Velocity lasts

Naps scratch firmaments
The woodland coils underground 895
Low although windswept

Two flotsams shall glide
Even if jade, the wave weeps 896
Brushes sense the grass

Underwater sleep
A path weeps beside one marsh 897
Swooning like noontime

Catnap fears its log
Observatory closes 898
The blue is tired

Distance tests few paths
Those limbs sense each hot whisper 899
Its green seashores boast

A wave licks the buoy
Although closing, shorelines push 900
Seaboards scratch the moss

Brush prefers midday
901 Both buoys touch a wild heat-snooze
One fixed eye relents

Groves touch surfaces
902 And residues float like naps
Science splits a hair

The wild twig ought rise
903 Each sand hides in a red dress
Brightnesses hidden

Chaff plants its darkness
904 Crossing tired surfaces
Some particles waft

Sleepy stems swish fast
905 Twigs must squash but grasses breathe
Bobbing lewd azures

Naps glues residues
906 Brushing ungold sediments
Plain, one snooze forgot

A drowsy brightness
907 But now branches wake, unstrong
Photography ends

Trash pats flotsam-lake
908 Few grasses last round blue eyes
Shame hides their color

Whiffs rush each zephyr
909 A grass dissects round the branch
Bugs dare compute paths

Both strands form brushes
More jumpy sparks hope for water 910
Blues verbalize more

Yellow shores list fast
Few limbs warn the strong sparkle 911
Weakful and yellow

Breeze fails underbrush
The snoozes scratch off smooth mites 912
The mosses quarrel

Two currents address
Who could jump in with the warmth 913
White and crystalline

Bark glides like fishes
Two roads scorch the green blanket 914
Nap can ignore it

Plants scrape the shoreline
Fashioning each afternoon 915
On indigo shores

Books read cottonwoods
Both weekends cut through water 916
Lit up by a breeze

Certain mites swish more
Preach mysteriously by moss 917
Green trashes must book

Both snoozes perceive
Carriages far below them 918
White swamps ought give pause

The deep waters hum
919 Calm, peaceful, but translucent
White shores could undress

Brush upsets darkness
920 Bark vanishes slow brushes
Eyes entertain them

Few twigs float on paths
921 One murk soothsays the flotsam
Wafts buttress upright

One wave carries sands
922 Cottonwoods bob their wild sleeps
And each plant must waft

Woods breathe the woodland
923 The head strengthens about suns
Mute though still happy

Bush sniffs its purpose
924 One scrap welcomes each smooth stem
A grass wavers, weak

Breeze breaks existence
925 Slow-moving, languid days end
The brightness of noon

Each bush queues the barks
926 Atmosphere dares knit blue darks
The woodland twigs rest

Darkness looks at clouds
927 Echoes fax, lest they dare watch
Existence returns

Those mosses shall reign
Residue helps them waver 928
Each large twig guards one

Wisps hoe each nothing
The fleck conveys the calm day 929
Blue and wet-yellow

Floors cork surfaces
Smooth, windswept, and estival 930
Wet and now languid

Billows glow above
Electric lakes sit helpless 931
Smooth existences

Brightness claims few twigs
Even if calm, one log parks 932
Its lit bark rolls well

Twig robs slumber-sky
A windswept trash glides each bush 933
And slow-moving sleep

Both breezes can rise
Drowsy flecks preach sleepily 934
Wild but faded

Swings float a brightness
The waters flash wet secrets 935
Eye, low across log

Pensive growths touch soon
Gold and torpid yet abstract 936
Lit and slow-moving

Branch frames surfaces
937 Marsh-murks drift yet still address
The round woodland swing

Those shorelines could swish
938 But still forcing, waters watch
Low underbrushes

Murk quits cottonwood
939 Snoozes roll across lit woods
Precipitates sink

Two yonders did stretch
940 Nonetheless strong, the moss weeps
Wet and now languid

Bug cheers existence
941 Lone twigs brush the wet low log
Their chaffs wonder it

Sways knot the flora
942 Summery, taming growths screw
Their gold heavens teach

Shores count what conveys
943 But still shrinking, insects launch
Snakes acquire more

Sleeps pass green darkness
944 The blankets inch past the lakes
Underbrushes breathe

These murks forgive silts
945 Their brightness eats the woods
Refrigerator

Suns push undergrowths
Flotsams blush through torpid logs 946
Each yawns wearily

A yellow jetsam
Though lakefront, slumbers shall thrive 947
While languid wood fights

Branch hovers surface
The slate preoccupation 948
Their gentle swishing

One gusty weekend
When twigs drown defiantly 949
A billow-wood drums

Growth grips underbrush
Two buoys scratch each weak surface 950
While hammocks reason

Flotsam flips its branch
The woodland leans with a snooze 951
Unlimpid grounds march

Tranquil branches sway
Pasting drowsy brightnesses 952
A low branch could rub

Knot fools crisp lagoons
The branch-sea moves between eyes 953
Their shut seaside puffs

More lakeshores confuse
Hot dares brush the wet cloud-twigs 954
Each blue becomes white

Brush spoils surprises
955 Soft, languid, still fantastic
Envisioning clouds

Moss tames oasis
956 The grass-log burns towards each sky
The wind snoozes too

Ponds stink with brightness
957 A bush bobs behind current
A particle pumps

One rabid silt-moss
958 These limbs watch a white darkness
The heat still needless

The gists couch flowers
959 Each insect beats above plants
And brightnesses cleave

The hot murk wafts up
960 Slumbers fall from the treetops
The birds buttress them

The mosses will conquer
961 Ribbons red from hammock finds
A windswept guesswork

Brightness moves its strand
962 Snoozes dream yet still ought sneak
Calm, the moss does squash

One distance must bob
963 Healing peaceful undergrowths
A hose fresh with silt

Wafts hasten ahead
One limpid experience 964
A cicada nods

Each eye wakes the log
The match swims between darkness 965
Paste flotsams generously

Lone shores propose yawns
Sun-heats pass by somber wafts 966
A bug though a marsh

A space dries the twigs
Firmament can deal calmness 967
Precipitates push

Some logs bake waters
Even if white, each marsh looks 968
White though now brushing

Lonely twigs rush more
One poplar clings since winter 969
Their bayfronts lament

Yawns dress residues
Both white blues swish the bushes 970
A mere beautybrush

One cloud casts the snooze
One voyage glides within dreams 971
One tree awakens

Glossy knots sew fast
Insects wait and sparkles gaze 972
Few lean lakeshores bless

Noons sneeze vacations
973 Abrasive, burly skies watch
Left limbs do powder

Waves bob and relent
974 Water must rest til morning
No snooze while windswept

One bush wafts breezes
975 Still jumping, blankets ought part
One sky but still calm

Darkness seeks two logs
976 Breezes branch by breezy whiffs
Brightness amasses

Flotsam ticks its sand
977 Few noons mug a wild sleep-brush
Their clouds diverge them

Heat can swish breeze-shore
978 Blinding lakes brush gleefully
Grass processes less

Each moss blots ices
979 These branch-paths touch to heaven
Substances dare rise

Grounds soar a slumber
980 Lone growths wonder at weak moss
Beneath tarns, surprise

One breeze boasts marshes
981 No brushes fix what putters
Snooze satisfies them

A cloud warns the logs
The lucid experience 982
Under brush, brightness

Hairs ride cicadas
A moss lives onto green bush 983
Slumbers solve one shore

A beauty shall lose
The log could smash beyond branch 984
Waggish, chaffs shelter

Mite brushes increase
More low suns flip with the path 985
Moss, gold within brush

Wisps cork residues
And still stuffing, branches teach 986
Aloneness lingers

Snooze lends particles
The moss receives the warm logs 987
The heat can pause them

One scrap would cross logs
No green woods pant down hot logs 988
Low, a log presses

Each tiny darkness
Thrusting among darknesses 989
Those surfaces glint

Each snooze plays brushes
Spread judgementally about 990
Naps diagnose them

The breeze drains the grass
991 A crystalline brightness trots
Up there, no one breathes

Those mosses murmur
992 Snoring windswept surfaces
Underbrushes grow

Logs brush darknesses
993 Wet, exposed, still somnolent
Vegetations change

An oasis says
994 Few branches move with signals
Teach regularly

One blanket dares lead
995 The shore round a pond inspires
Yellow and ready

Waves grip cottonwoods
996 A grass would branch towards the knot
Activities brush

Languid blues trace fast
997 Surfaces rule behind gists
Jade although warming

Lace glides its surface
998 Some marshes peek what did couch
Utterly peaceful

A branch sorts its stem
999 Yet still seaside, branches cross
White existences

Moss veers to darkness
Translucent, sleepy whiffs scorch 1000
Crisp naps could emerge

Sleeps float on hammocks
The drowsy groves chase each breeze 1001
Marsh amasses them

Certain heads clear well
One billow shades over feet 1002
Black even if plain

Floor feels what tips well
Smooth, tranquil, while indigo 1003
Strong and estival

Phobic cicada
Twigs did absorb blue hammocks 1004
Feeble although proud

Both gold swings would charge
More sways pause one wild snooze 1005
From bush, flotsam boasts

Shores brush a setting
Atmospheres swish within them 1006
Calm and summery

Each underbrush combs
One lakefront vegetation 1007
The water is blue

Each grass hosts a branch
The nap dares gaze at darkness 1008
Carelessly torpid

Grass cures backwaters
1009 A blue-eyed lake blinks at shoal
Mites examine skin

White marsh-woods breathing
1010 Residues work against it
Sky fears its poplar

Moss bobs with brightness
1011 Sun thaws the nothings that please
Weak flowers float bugs

One face knits, quiet
1012 Eyes ought challenge the brush-bugs
The white one chatters

Plants release whispers
1013 Growing arrogantly up
The logs move elsewhere

An unkempt lakefront
1014 Clean and aloof and needy
Touching tenderly

A hot afternoon
1015 The important feeling snacks
Gardens close the snooze

Noontime brightnesses
1016 Two slow eyes see more colors
Patios await

The heat must swish limbs
1017 One moss secures onto limbs
Evolutionist

The oasis rubs
Crisp and shunting while electric 1018
Its electric bark

Water-fervors cut
Some slumbers touch what injects 1019
Shrill logs did soften

Drowsy hairs sign off
The lake labels the dirt floor 1020
Frail and indigo

The cloud spits azures
Both sleep-twigs load their advice 1021
A picnic meddles

Trash pastes firmaments
Snake-buoys stretch as drowsy towns 1022
Abaft, currents scratch

Sky enlists seashore
No gusty suns face the grass 1023
Lush and thinkable

Moss tours enclosures
Pensive bugs act noisily 1024
Grass must surprise it

About the Author

Ian Bogost is a videogame designer, researcher, and critic. He holds a professorship at the Georgia Institute of Technology, where he also directs the graduate program in digital media. In addition to his writings and independent games, Bogost also makes games about social and political issues in his role as founding partner of Persuasive Games LLC. Find him online at http://www.bogost.com.

A Slow Year System Requirements

The CD-ROM accompanying this book contains installers for *A Slow Year* for both Windows and Mac. The following system requirements apply:

Windows:	*Mac:*
Windows XP, Vista, or 7	Mac OS X 10.5+
OpenGL-capable graphics	OpenGL-capable graphics
5 megabytes free disk space	17 megabytes free disk space

By installing, you agree to the terms of the software license agreement, which appears below.

Software License Agreement